BRAUDE'S TREASURY

of WIT and HUMOR

BRAUDE'S TREASURY of WIT and HUMOR

by Jacob M. Braude

PRENTICE-HALL, INC.
Englewood Cliffs, N. J.

Braude's Treasury of Wit and Humor, by Jacob M. Braude

LIBRARY OF CONGRESS
CATALOG CARD NUMBER: 64-14542

Reward Edition . . . . . November, 1973

Fifth Printing . . . . . August, 1979

PRINTED IN THE UNITED STATES OF AMERICA

By the Same Author
and the Same Publisher

SPEAKER'S ENCYCLOPEDIA OF STORIES,
QUOTATIONS AND ANECDOTES

BRAUDE'S SECOND ENCYCLOPEDIA OF STORIES,
QUOTATIONS AND ANECDOTES

BRAUDE'S HANDBOOK OF HUMOR
FOR ALL OCCASIONS

NEW TREASURY OF STORIES
FOR EVERY SPEAKING AND WRITING OCCASION

SPEAKER'S ENCYCLOPEDIA OF HUMOR

LIFETIME SPEAKER'S ENCYCLOPEDIA

SPEAKER'S DESK BOOK OF QUIPS, QUOTES AND ANECDOTES

Every man who knows how to read has it in his power to magnify himself, to multiply the ways in which he exists, to make his life full, significant and interesting.
—ALDOUS HUXLEY

INTRODUCTION

While primarily slanted to the needs of the public speaker, this book can be a source of pleasure and entertainment to the man and woman who may be called upon to make a public utterance. There are hundreds of anecdotes, jokes and stories which follow that can be used over and over again to help you scintillate in your daily conversation. They comprise some of the best of thousands of items which I have managed to collect during the course of some fifty years of reading, clipping and filing.

I myself have dipped into this material literally thousands of times while preparing my own public speeches and writings and it is without reservation that I recommend it to the reader for the same purpose because in making my selection, I have always asked myself, "Can this be used with effect upon an audience and does it help to make a point that I am trying to put over?"

All of us have had the experience of trying desperately to reach back into the recesses of our memory for some story or anecdote to illustrate a given point and all too often that memory has failed us or has come up with an unsatisfactory substitute. In this book I have tried to build a never-failing addition to one's memory and have undertaken to make it readily accessible through the minutely detailed index which is part of the book itself. Here one will find titles, subject matter and also key words, which provide broad paths from which one can pinpoint the answer to a particular speaking or writing need.

Whoever makes use of this volume for the primary purpose for which it is intended is like the young man who always enters a movie theater with his eyes tightly shut; this, in turn, thereafter enables him to see in the dark and to find his seat. It has been my observation that too many public speakers seem to close their eyes to the need of brightening up their material with pertinent, illustrative anecdotes. The material in this book will be found to glow in the darkness of a dull or colorless presentation and thus bring it to life once again.

It is a good policy never to put one's listening audience in the position of the diner who asked of his waiter: "What have I done that they have kept me on bread and water for two hours?" With the material in this book you will be able to give your audience a gourmet's thought diet by flavoring your ideas with the wisdom and humor of others—always directly pertinent to the issue at hand.

With these few words I leave you on your own with the wish that you have happy hunting as you set forth in search for the story or anecdote that "just fits." My relationship with the material in this book is pretty much like that of the young lad who was riding horseback with his girl friend. As they stopped to rest, the two horses rubbed necks affectionately.

"Ah, me," said the lad, "that's what I'd like to do, too."

"Go ahead," said the girl, "it's *your* horse."

And I say to you about the material that follows: "Go ahead, friend. It's *yours* now. Read it, use it, and enjoy it."

CONTENTS

A

Absent-mindedness

1. "Jack's getting terribly absent-minded of late. Why just the other day he kissed a woman by mistake."

"Thought it was his wife, eh?"

"No, that's just it. It was his wife."

2. An absent-minded man tied a string around his finger in the early afternoon to remind him when he got home that there was something he wanted to be sure to do. After dinner, while reading his paper, he noticed the string but couldn't remember why he put it there. He decided if he sat up long enough, the reason for the string would come to him. And surely enough, around two o'clock in the morning it did—he wanted to go to bed early that night.

Accuracy

3. A stranger entered the building and asked a boy standing in the lobby, "Can you tell me where Mr. Smith lives?"

The lad smiled and replied pleasantly, "Yes, sir. I'll show you."

Six flights up the boy pointed out a room as that belonging to Mr. Smith. The man pounded on the door repeatedly and, after no response, commented, "He's not here."

"Oh, no, sir," replied the boy. "Mr. Smith was downstairs waiting in the lobby."

4. A tourist was visiting New Mexico. While gazing at the dinosaur bones that were everywhere, he met an old Indian who acted as an unofficial guide.

"How old are these bones?" asked the tourist.

"Exactly one hundred million and three years old," was the Indian's reply.

"How can you be so definite?" inquired the tourist.

"Oh, a geologist told me they were one hundred million years old," replied the Indian, "and that was exactly three years ago."

Achievement

5. *Bob:* "Can you do anything that other people can't?"
Herb: "Why, yes. I can read my own handwriting."

Admiration

6. A young American woman stood before Beethoven's piano in a Vienna museum. Presently she struck off a few discordant notes. "I suppose," she said to the attendant, "that many noted musicians have inspected this instrument."

"Oh, yes," replied the man. "Recently Paderewski was here."

"Paderewski!" exclaimed the visitor. "Certainly he must have played something wonderful."

"On the contrary; he did not feel worthy to touch it."

Advertising

7. *Want ad:* Secretary wants job; no bad habits; willing to learn.

8. If advertising can be accused of making people live beyond their means, so can matrimony.

9. A manufacturer said he was going to cut down on his advertising to save money. To which his salesman replied: "You might as well stop your watch to save time."

10. A ketchup company in Canada ran a series of advertisements that really rocked the country. The ad showed a man dining in a restaurant about to cut into a steak; the pretty waitress was serving a bottle of ketchup. The blazing headline on the ad read: "He gets it downtown—why don't you give it to him at home?"

11. A man who lives in the suburbs of Los Angeles and who works in the advertising department of a large metropolitan newspaper had never been able to figure out the deferential attitude, bordering on awe, of the children in the block towards him. Recently, he was walking around the block for a little stroll and he came upon a group of little boys discussing the newest American satellite as it hurtled through orbital space around the earth. As he paused to say hello to the youngsters, everything suddenly became clear when one of the boys said to him: "Are you really a space salesman?"

Age

12. The age of some women is like the speedometer on a used car—you know it's set back but you don't know how far.

13. *Teacher:* "How old would a person be who was born in 1920?"
Smart pupil: "Man or woman?"

14. The judge pounded his gavel for the court to come to order, then turned to the woman in the witness box.

"The witness will please state her age," he ordered, "after which she will be sworn in."

15. *Conductor:* "You will have to pay fare for that child, lady. He's over twelve."

Passenger: "How can he be over twelve when I've only been married ten years."

Conductor: "Lady, I just collect fares—not confessions."

16. A pretty girl came to a roulette table at Las Vegas with a $100 bill and explained to a group of gentlemen admirers that she could not decide which number to bet it on.

"Why don't you play it on your age?" one of the men suggested.

"That's a good idea—I'll do it," the girl said, and she placed the $100 on 22. The wheel spun and finally came to a stop at 28.

"Oh, *no!!*" the girl gasped and fell to the floor in a faint.

17. "Your name, please?" asked the registration officer.

"Matilda Brown," answered the woman.

"And your age?" he pursued.

"Have the Misses Hill next door, given you their ages?" she asked, hesitantly.

"No," said the officer.

"Well, then, I'm the same age as they."

"That will do," said the officer. Then, proceeding to fill out the form, he wrote, "Matilda Brown, as old as the Hills."

Aging

18. You're getting old when you don't care where your wife goes, just so you don't have to go along.

19. A white-haired old man approached his doctor and said: "Doctor, I'm slowly going nuts over women. Is there any way to speed it up?"

20. Careful grooming and a smooth paint job will take 20 years off a woman's true age. But you can't fool a long flight of stairs.

21. In the village post office a stranger saw the local patriarch sitting on a flour barrel, whistling. A bystander informed him that the old fellow already had passed his hundredth birthday. Impressed, the man exclaimed, "That's amazing!"

"We don't see nothin' amazin' about it 'round here," was the laconic reply. "All he's done is grow old—and he took longer to do that than most people would!"

22. It is said that when Konrad Adenauer, former West German Chancellor, was laid up with the grippe, he chafed at his doctor and said he had to get better because he was scheduled to make an official trip abroad.

"I'm not a magician," said the doctor. "I can't make you young again."

To which Adenauer is reported to have replied: "I'm not asking that. I don't want to become young again; all I want is to go on getting old."

23. Sir Winston Churchill, whose fondness for drink was well known, was scheduled to make a speech before a small gathering.

The chairman introduced him by saying: "If all the spirits consumed by Sir Winston were poured into this room, it would reach up to here on the wall."

He drew a line with his finger at about level with his eyes.

Churchill got up to speak. He glanced at the imaginary line on the wall. He looked up at the ceiling, and made a mathematical calculation with his fingers. Then he sighed and said, "Ah, so much to be done, and so little time in which to do it."

America—Americanism

24. If you want your father to take care of you, that's paternalism. If you want your mother to take care of you, that's maternalism. If you want Uncle Sam to take care of you, that's Socialism. If you want your comrades to take care of you, that's Communism. But if you want to take care of yourself, that's Americanism.

Ancestry

25. "I want a dog of which I can be proud," said Mrs. Newlyrich. "Does that one have a good pedigree?"

"Lady," declared the kennel owner, "if he could talk, he wouldn't speak to either of us."

26. The lady was trying to impress those at the party. "My family's ancestry is very old," she said. "It dates back to the days of King John of England." Then turning to a lady sitting quietly in a corner she asked condescendingly: "How old is your family, my dear?"

"Well," said the woman with a quiet smile, "I can't really say. All our family records were lost in the Flood."

Anger

27. A man is never in worse company than when he flies into a rage and is beside himself.

Antique—Antiques

28. A lady, traveling in a set determined to outdo one another in their search for antiques, one day called upon the leader and excitedly remarked: "I came across something marvelous. An archaeologist friend sent me the very cup from which Socrates drank the hemlock."

"Are you sure it's authentic?" gasped the pace-setter.

"Authentic?" repeated the woman. "Why when they dug it up it was marked 350 B.C."

Appearances

29. A man was driving to town one morning with his wife. The weather was hot and the windows were rolled up. "Honey," he said, "please open the windows."

"Are you crazy!" she exclaimed. "And let our neighbors driving in the next lane know our car isn't air-conditioned?"

30. Two girls at the beach were admiring the passing scene, which included an athletic chap, who was strutting his best.

"That's my kind," said one.

"Well, I don't know," the other replied. "I had a friend who married a man who owned a two-car garage, but he just keeps a bicycle in it."

Approval

31. It was a blistering-hot afternoon as the old senator stood on the rear platform of a campaign train orating at length to the uneasy crowd of voters gathered at the railroad station. Before he had completed his speech, the train started to pull out. Immediately the crowd broke into applause, accompanied by cheering and shouting.

With the shouts fading in the distance, the senator poured himself a shot of bourbon and remarked to a reporter: "You know something? I'm not sure whether they were applauding me or the engineer."

Arithmetic

32. Several young clerical workers were riding down in the elevator for their coffee break. Forgetting completely the warnings of her high school math teacher, one chic little number complained: "That job I got. Is it ever strict? If the total is wrong, it's all wrong!"

33. "When are you going back to school, Tom?"
"I'm not going back, 'cause my teacher's gone crazy."
"Gone crazy?"
"Yes. One day she told us that four and one are five, and today she says that two and three make five."

34. "I can't figure it out," said the small boy trying to get his father to help him with his arithmetic. "If a carpenter was paid $3 a day, how much did he earn in four days?"
"No wonder you can't figure it out," replied the father. "That's not arithmetic—that's ancient history."

35. The harried coach pleaded with the professor who had flunked his prize tackle to give the boy another chance. Finally the professor agreed and did give his boy a special makeup exam.
The next day the coach again anxiously queried the professor. "How did Jones do?"
"I'm sorry," said the professor. "It's hopeless. Look at this
. . . 7 x 5 = 33."
"But gosh, Professor," said the coach, "give him a break. He only missed it by one."

Armed Forces

36. If you think old soldiers just fade away, try getting into your old Army uniform.

37. *Johnnie:* "I would rather be a general than a private. Generals don't have to fight for their medals."

38. A soldier leaving an army base was overheard saying to a comrade: "This has got to be love at first sight. I'm on an eight-hour pass."

39. *Supply officer:* "How does your new uniform fit?"
Recruit: "The jacket isn't bad, but the trousers are just a little loose around the armpits."

40. *Postmaster:* "I'm sorry, but I can't cash this money order unless you have some identification. Have you friends in camp?"
Soldier: "Not me: I'm the camp's bugler."

41. The sergeant was explaining some important points to a squad of recruits on the rifle range.
"This type of bullet will penetrate two feet of solid wood," he said. "So remember to keep your heads down."

42. "Look here, private, this man beside you on this fatigue detail is doing twice the work you are."
"I know, sarge. That's what I've been telling him for the last hour, but he won't slow down."

43. The major who received a complaint about the issue of bread snapped angrily, "If Napoleon had had that bread in Russia, he would have eaten it with the greatest relish."
"Yes, sir," spoke up the sergeant, "but it was fresh then."

44. The draftee was awakened roughly by his platoon sergeant after the rookie's first night in the army barracks.
"It's four-thirty!" roared the sergeant.
"Four-thirty!" gasped the recruit. "Man, you'd better get to bed. We've got a big day tomorrow!"

45. An officer in the South Pacific who had been overseas sixteen months received a letter from his wife telling about a prayer their four-year-old daughter made: "Dear Lord, please send me a baby brother so we will have something to surprise Daddy with when he gets home."

46. An applicant for employment gave as his reason for

leaving his previous job, which was that of a temporary sorter at the post office: "Done all the work."

He had also served in the Army, and to the formal question: "Why did you leave the Forces?" he replied: "Won the War."

47. A naval officer fell overboard. He was rescued by a deck hand. The officer asked how he could reward him.

"The best way, sir," said the deck hand, "is to say nothing about it. If the other fellows knew I'd pulled you out, they'd chuck me in."

48. A sergeant in charge of the new recruits ordered: "Men, when I blow the whistle, I want you to shoot at will."

At that moment one very frightened young man ran across the grounds out of sight.

"Who was that? Where's he going?" bellowed the sergeant.

"That was Will," replied one of the recruits.

49. Sergeant-Major's golden rules for new recruits detailed for duty in the Officers' Mess:

"If it moves, salute it.

If it doesn't move, sweep it up.

If it's too big to sweep up, pick it up.

If it's too big to pick up, paint it."

50. The old colonel had put in forty long years under Army routine, and now he was being retired. He took his orderly with him as a servant, and gave him strict instructions:

"Now, George, each morning at five o'clock sharp you wake me up and say, 'Time for the parade, sir,' and then I'll say, 'Damn the parade!' and turn over and go back to sleep."

51. An Army marksman passed through a small town and saw evidence of amazing shooting. On trees, walls, fences, and barns were numerous bull's-eyes with the bullet hole in the exact center. He asked to meet the remarkable marksman.

The man turned out to be the village idiot. "This is the most wonderful marksmanship I've ever seen," said the Army man. "How in the world do you do it?"

"Easy as pie. I shoot first and draw the circle afterwards."

52. "Now watch out for the colonel, because he's coming to inspect the post," said the sergeant, as he marched off and left O'Brien to his first outpost duty. After an hour the sergeant returned. "Colonel been here yet?" he asked.

O'Brien saying "No," the sergeant again departed for an hour, returning with the same query.

Then, at last, the colonel did appear.

"Do you know who I am?" he asked O'Brien.

"Shure, an' I don't at all," replied the recruit.

"I am the colonel."

"Faith, an' you'll catch it, then! The sergeant's been asking fer you twice already."

53. The lady was not aware that her drive had carried her into an army maneuvers area. As she approached a small bridge, a sentry stopped her and said, "Sorry, but you can't drive across this bridge. It has just been demolished." Leaving her dumbfounded, for the bridge was in perfect repair, he walked off.

As she sat pondering the possibility that the sentry was insane, another soldier approached. "Young man," she asked, "can you tell me any reason why I can't cross that bridge?"

"Lady," he replied soberly, "I can't tell you a thing. I've been dead for two days."

54. Two harassed-looking privates were staggering across the barrack square from the direction of the kitchens with a huge steaming cauldron slung between them. The most officious, most interfering officer in the whole regiment spotted them from his window and straightaway sallied forth. "Hi, there—you men—put that down." They did so. "Get me a ladle," ordered the officer. "B-b-but, sir——" stammered one of the privates. "Don't query an order," snapped the officer. "Do as you are told. Get me a ladle." A ladle was duly obtained. The officer dipped it into the cauldron, brought it out full, blew on the contents, swallowed them. His face changed. "Call that soup?" he demanded, fiercely. "N-n-no, sir," came the stammering reply, "it's the water we've just done the washing-up in."

55. A draftee on his way to training camp asked another draftee. "Do you happen to have a match?"

"Sure," was the second draftee's reply. "But I'm making sure not to give you any."

"But why?" was the startled query from the first recruit.

"Well," said the second, "we'll get to talking, and if we get to talking, we'll wind up as buddies. And if we're buddies, we'll get into the same tent and the same squad; then we'll both volunteer to go for special missions. Maybe we'll even get a dangerous night job; and we'll have to use flashlights. And if the flashlights should happen to go out some dark night in enemy territory, I sure don't want to be stranded with someone who doesn't even carry matches!"

Art

56. The newly rich woman was going through a "culture" routine and at this particular moment was standing in front of a painting at New York's famous Metropolitan Museum. It was a beautiful oil of a ragged but happy vagabond.

"Well!" exclaimed the woman indignantly. "How do you like that? Too broke to buy a decent suit of clothes, but he can afford to go out and get his portrait painted."

57. A tiny but dignified old lady was among a group looking at an art exhibition in a newly opened gallery recently. Suddenly one contemporary painting caught her eye.

"What on earth," she inquired of the artist standing nearby, "is that?"

He smiled condescendingly. "That, my dear lady, is supposed to be a mother and her child."

"Well, then," snapped the little old lady, "why isn't it?"

Art, Modern

58. Two teenagers on a tour of a modern art gallery found themselves alone in a room of modern sculpture. Staring at the twisted pipes, broken glass, and tangled shapes, one of them said, "Let's get out of here before they accuse us of wrecking this place."

59. An American GI who met Pablo Picasso in Paris told the artist that he didn't like modern paintings because they weren't realistic. Picasso made no immediate reply. A few minutes later the soldier showed him a snapshot of his girl friend.

"My word," said Picasso, "is she *really* as small as all that?"

Atomic age

60. When the lady who was making out the application came to the little square marked "Age," she did not hesitate. She simply wrote: "Atomic."

61. A group of atomic scientists held a convention at Las Vegas, and one of the professors spent all of his free time at the gambling tables. A couple of his colleagues were discussing their friend's weakness.

"Fenwick gambles as if there were no tomorrow," one said.

"Maybe," commented the other, "he knows something."

Attention

62. A professor who had taught for many years was counseling a young teacher. "You will discover," he said, "that in nearly every class, there will be a youngster eager to argue. Your first impulse will be to silence him, but I advise you to think carefully before doing so. He probably is the only one listening."

Attire

63. The clothes that make a woman break a man.

64. *She:* "The contralto certainly has a large repertoire." *He:* "Yes and that tight dress sure shows it off."

65. A woman wears a sweater to accentuate the positive and a girdle to eliminate the negative.

66. Mother had bought father a new tie for his birthday. "I wonder what would go best with it," she asked, after he had opened the package.

Father eyed the violet-colored horror, and exclaimed, "A beard!"

67. Down South for a visit, the young Yankee made a date with a local lovely. When he called for her at her home, she was clad in a low-cut, tight-fitting gown. He remarked, "That's a beautiful dress."

"Sho 'nough?" she drawled.

"It sure does."

68. A rather stout woman visited her foot doctor. After he pried her foot loose from a dainty shoe, he asked her what her trouble was.

"It seems my feet are always swollen," she complained. "I wonder what causes this."

The doctor glanced at her feet, then at the shoes. "Well," he mused, "it could be pride in accomplishing the impossible."

69. The wife who could not attend the banquet with her husband began questioning him about what the women wore to the gala affair.

Somewhat exasperated he finally replied, "They didn't wear anything, as far as I know."

"Do you mean," she demanded, "that women came there with no clothes on at all?"

"They didn't have on any clothes above the table," he assured her, "and I didn't dare look under it."

Authorship

70. "Why do you insist on calling him a pharmacist when you know he's an author?"

"Because every book he writes is a drug on the market."

71. A prisoner in a state penitentiary wrote a crime story and sent it to a magazine editor with this note: "The facts in this story are true, only the names have been changed to protect the guilty."

72. Novelist Sinclair Lewis was to lecture a group of college students who planned literary careers. Lewis opened his talk by saying:

"How many of you really intend to be writers?"

All hands went up.

"In that case," said Lewis, returning his notes to his pocket, "my advice to you is to go home and write."

With that, he left the room.

73. Heywood Broun hated ghostwritten political speeches. His comment was that usually they failed to reflect the personality or the convictions of the individuals who delivered them.

It was during a newsmen's dinner that President Harding delivered a real Websteronian oration loaded with outlandish clichés and pompous language. It was completely out of character. As the polite applause died down after the President had finished, Broun leaped from his seat and cried:

"Author! Author!"

Bachelorhood

74. The only thing worse than being a bachelor is being a bachelor's son.

75. *Prospective employee:* "Just why do you want a married man to work for you rather than a bachelor?"
Boss: "The married men don't get so upset if I yell at them."

76. "I was sorry to hear that your brother passed on," one old classmate consoled another at a reunion. "Had he finished his education?"
"No," said the other. "He died a bachelor."

77. The bachelor's attractive new housekeeper tiptoed into the study and asked apologetically, "Sir, shall I clean your stove and sweep your porch now?"
"Margie," said the bachelor, "in this house we are all for one and one for all. You do not say 'your stove' or 'your porch' or 'your chair.' Instead you say 'our stove' or 'our porch' or 'our chair.'"
That evening Margie served a spendid dinner to the bachelor and his boss and the boss' daughter, whom the bachelor was anxious to impress.
Margie was late in serving the last course and she rushed

into the dining room and excitedly announced: "I'm sorry I was late, sir, but I was upstairs chasing a mouse from under 'our bed.' "

Backfire

78. A young man looking for a seat on a crowded train walked to the last car and cried in a loud voice: "All change here. This car isn't going."

With exclamations the passengers cleared the car, and the young man sat down, made himself comfortable and waited— and waited.

Finally the station agent appeared. "You the smart young man who said this car wasn't going?"

"Yep," replied the clever one.

"Well," said the agent, "it isn't. You sounded so much like a director, they just uncoupled the car."

79. An Englishman, a Welshman and a Scotsman were left legacies by a friend on condition that each should put five pounds in his coffin.

The Englishman put in a five-pound note. The Welshman also put in five pounds which he had borrowed from the Englishman.

The Scotsman took out the two five-pound notes and put in a cheque for fifteen pounds, payable to bearer.

Three days later he was astonished to learn that the cheque had been presented and cashed. The undertaker was an Irishman.

Baldness

80. *Small boy in barber's chair:* "I want my hair cut like my daddy's—with a hole on top."

81. There are three ways in which a man can wear his hair: parted, unparted, departed.

Bank—Banks—Banking

82. *Office boy:* "I think I know what's wrong with this country!"

Bank executive: "And what's that, son?"

Office boy: "We're trying to run America with only one vice-president."

83. A wealthy Texas oilman cashed a huge personal check which came back from the bank with "INSUFFICIENT FUNDS" stamped across its face. Beneath the stamped words was the handwritten notation: "Not you . . . us."

84. Wanting to borrow some money to make a six-month tour of Europe, a man went to the bank where he had done business for years. The bank refused the loan.

He went to another bank and obtained the loan without any difficulty. Then he bought a five-pound fish, had it wrapped, and put it in his safe-deposit box at the first bank as he joyfully left town for six months.

85. The burglars had tied and gagged the bank cashier after extracting the combination to the safe and had herded the other employees into a separate room under guard. After they rifled the safe and were about to leave the cashier made desperate pleading noises through the gag. Moved by curiosity one of the burglars loosened the gag.

"Please!" whispered the cashier, "take the books, too: I'm $6,500 short."

Barber—Barber shop

86. "Your dog likes to watch you cut hair, doesn't he?"

"It ain't that. Sometimes I snip off a bit of ear."

87. *Customer:* "I want a close shave."
Barber: "You just had one."
Customer: "How's zat?"
Barber: "That big guy who walked in just as you took your hand off the manicurist's knee is her husband."

88. A man walked into the barber's and asked for a shave. The barber's young assistant spoke up: "May I try shaving him? It'll be good practice."

"All right—go ahead," replied his boss doubtfully. "But be careful. Don't cut yourself."

89. A barber with a bad case of "morning after the night before" shakes nicked the customer he was shaving. The customer commented, "You see what too much liquor will do to you?"

"Yeah," replied the barber, "it sure makes your skin tender."

90. Sam, the barber, seemed a little jumpy and it made his customer nervous. "Sam," he said, "what happens if you cut a customer? Does the boss get sore?"

"Yes, he does," Sam replied. "He makes us pay a dollar for every cut we give a customer—but I don't care, I had a good day at the races yesterday."

Bargain—Bargains

91. *Fond parent to little boy:* "How much is two and two, son?"
Little boy: "Six."
Fond parent: "No, son, that's wrong. The answer is four."
Little boy: "I know what the answer is, father, but I just wanted to hear you bargain."

92. *Line dispatcher:* "Say, young lady, will you please show me some er—er black lace unmentionables?"

Cute salesgirl: "Surely, sir. Here are several lovely pieces. And it might be of interest to you to know that this is the only place you can touch these for anywhere near the price."

93. An old lady stepped up to the ticket window in the railway station and asked, "How much is a ticket to Cleveland?"

"That's ten dollars and seventy-nine cents," replied the agent.

The old lady turned to the little girl beside her and said, "I guess we may as well buy our tickets here. I've asked at all these windows, and they are the same price everywhere."

Beauty

94. If all brides are beautiful, where do so many ugly women come from?

95. Two businessmen were relaxing on the beach at Miami. "You know," one began, "what does everyone see in Elizabeth Taylor? Take away her hair, her lips, her eyes, and her figure—and what've you got?" The other businessman grunted. "My wife," he said sadly.

Behavior

96. Little monkeys grow up to be big monkeys; little pigs grow up to be big pigs; but man, wonderful man, can grow up to be either.

97. "I noticed that your daughter didn't get home until two this morning. My daughter, Shirley, was in by midnight."

"I know, but you see, my daughter walked home."

98. A Broadway playboy decided to reform. The first week he cut out cigarettes. The second week he cut out booze. The third week he cut out dames. And the fourth week he cut out paper dolls.

99. *Millie:* "I went out last night with a Southerner. He took me to dinner and dancing and was a perfect gentleman. Then he took me home in a cab."

Lillie: "What happened then?"

Millie: "He got a bit Northern."

100. A newspaper was running a competition to discover the most high-principled, sober, well-behaved local citizen. Among the entries came one which read:

"I don't smoke, touch intoxicants or gamble. I am faithful to my wife and never look at another woman. I am hard-working, quiet and obedient. I never go to the movies or the theater, and I go to bed early every night and rise with the dawn. I attend chapel regularly every Sunday without fail.

"I've been like this for the past three years. But just wait until next spring, when they let me out of here!"

Bet—Bets—Betting. See also Gambling

101. And then there's the touching story of the young man who said to his girl, "I bet you wouldn't marry me."

The story goes that she not only called his bet but raised him five.

102. The bookie slowly counted out the money into the old lady's wrinkled hands.

"Lady," he said, "I just don't understand. However did you manage to pick the winner?"

The old lady patted her white locks in place. She looked a little bewildered.

"Really," she said, "I don't know myself. I just stick a pin in the paper and, well, there it is."

The bookie took a deep breath.

"That's all very well, lady," he cried. "But how on earth did you manage to pick four winners yesterday afternoon?"

"Oh," replied the old lady, "that was easy. You see, I used a fork."

Bible, The

103. A woman was mailing the Old Family Bible to a brother in a distant city.

Postal clerk: "Does this package contain anything breakable?"

Lady: "Only the Ten Commandments."

Blame

104. Every man needs a wife because there are a number of things that go wrong that one can't blame on the government.

105. A government census-taker was questioning an old-timer about his home town. "How many people live in this town?" he wanted to know.

"'Bout four thousand people and it's been that way for twenty-five years," was the reply.

"You mean to tell me," said the census-taker, "that there were four thousand people here twenty-five years ago and only four thousand now? Haven't any people moved in—any babies been born here?"

"There sure have been babies born," cackled the old-timer. "Trouble is, that every time a baby is born, somebody leaves town."

Boastfulness

106. Composing a letter to the president of the firm, which he felt he so ably represented, the egotistical young salesman dictated to a stenographer:

"I feel that you should know, sir, that in order to obtain the above-mentioned contract, I found it necessary to employ every ounce of my personal charm and magnetism, my diplomacy and flawless tact. However, I am now pleased to report that my untiring efforts were crowned with success."

Gently the steno asked, "Crowtation marks on that last paragraph?"

107. An old master sergeant, a veteran of three wars, was hard put to keep a brash teenage recruit in his place. Although the youngster bragged, he had a disconcerting knack of making good his boasts.

Marched to the rifle range, he announced that he was the best shot in the rookie unit—and lived up to it by outshooting the other recruits by a large margin. That night in the barracks, everyone suffered through his detailed account of how "I set a new range record."

Turning to his sergeant, the boastful youngster remarked: "Bet you didn't shoot that well when you first joined up, sarge."

After a pause, the sergeant replied: "No, son, I didn't. But when I first shot, there was somebody shooting back."

108. Several hunters were sitting around bragging about the dogs they owned. Noting that an elderly native was listening intently, they laid it on thick.

"Take my setter," said one man. "When I send him to the store for eggs, he refuses to accept them unless they're fresh. What a nose that dog has!"

"That's nothing," boasted another. "My springer goes out for cigars and refuses to accept any but my favorite brand. Not only that, he won't smoke any until he gets home and I offer him one."

"Say, old-timer," said another man turning to the native, "did you ever hear of any dogs as smart as ours?"

"Just one—my brother's dog," was the reply. "I think he's a bit smarter."

"How?" he was asked.

"Well," replied the native, "he runs the store where your dogs trade."

Book—Books

109. Have you heard about the Pullman porter who just finished reading his first book? It's about Berth Control.

110. The student approached the desk of the librarian and began searching her handbag for a note she had taken in class. Not finding it, she said hastily, "I want to take out the book called *The Red Boat*."

The library assistant came back to her after a few minutes and said, "I'm sorry but we do not have a book by that title."

"I must have made a mistake," the girl replied. "I believe it was *The Scarlet Launch*."

Again the library assistant came back and this time, trying to be helpful, suggested, "Could it be *The Scarlet Letter* by Hawthorne that you want?"

"No. It's not about a letter. It's about a boat," the girl said. And then her face brightened as she found her notes. "I have it written down," she spoke happily. "It is the *Ruby Yacht* by a man named Omar something or other."

Borrowing

111. *Prospective borrower to banker:* "Now I'll need two thousand more . . . I bet my associate two grand that you'd turn me down."

112. *Husband:* "Darling, don't you think you're being a wee bit extravagant? You've had four electric fans running all day."

Bride: "Don't worry about it, dearest. They're not our fans; I borrowed them from the neighbors."

113. A fellow was endeavoring to borrow some money from a friend. The friend wanted to know why he didn't use his own money, and the fellow explained that everything he had was in a joint account. "But you can draw money from a joint account," volunteered his friend.

"Not this joint account," explained the financially destitute husband. "Our joint account is in the name of my wife and her mother."

Brevity

114. The cub reporter was told to keep his copy short and stick to the bare facts. Sent on his first accident story, he turned in this copy:

"S. White looked up the elevator shaft to see if the car was on its way down. It was. Age 45."

115. The lesson in newspaper work is constantly "Be brief!" If that order can be given picturesquely, so much the better and it will not be forgotten.

A certain beginner in journalism picked up in a southern town what seemed to him a "big story." He hurried to the telegraph office and queried the editor of his newspaper: "Column story on ——. Shall I send?"

The answer arrived promptly: "Send 600 words."

This to the enthusiastic correspondent was depressing. "Can't be told in less than 1,200," he wired back.

Then came this reply: "Story of creation of world told in 600. Try it."

Business

116. An executive who is a great believer in efficiency hung up a sign in his office one day last week. It read: "Do it now."

Within 24 hours, the cashier bolted with the contents of the safe, his stenographer eloped with his eldest son, the office boy threw the ink bottle into the electric fan, and the whole office force took the afternoon off.

117. A man walked into a dress shop and asked the proprietor how business was.

"Terrible!" he complained. "It's so bad, why I only sold one dress yesterday. And today it's even worse."

"How could it be worse?" asked his friend.

"Today she returned the dress she bought yesterday," wailed the proprietor.

118. A candy store operator was bemoaning the sad fate that had overtaken him. "I was a hard-working clerk, earning a mere ten dollars a week," he told his clergyman, "when, like so many ill-advised young men, I fell in with shady characters and felt compelled to gamble."

"Ah," sympathized the cleric, "and the temptation cost you all your hard-accumulated savings!"

"No," said the man. "I won—and like a damned fool bought this lousy candy store."

C

Card-playing. See also Gambling

119. Looks are sometimes deceiving. The man with a vacant look may have a full house.

120. The policeman stopped a man going down the street clad in a barrel.

"Are you a poker player?" he asked.

"No," the man replied, "but I just left some fellows who are."

121. The zoo keeper received an indignant complaint that the monkeys were playing poker and a warning that he should do something about it right away.

"That's all right," he soothed. "They're only playing for peanuts."

122. It was during a bridge game that a shapely girl felt a foot run up and down the calf of her leg. She looked at the other three players, all men, and then snarled:

"If that's my husband, I bid three no trump. If it's one of you other guys, he's gonna get a punch right in the nose!"

123. At 3:00 A.M., the cautious husband silently inserted his key in the front door, but his wife was on hand to greet him.

"Hah!" she cried. "Three o'clock! I suppose you're going to tell me you've been out somewhere holding a sick friend's hand."

"Well," said the man sadly, "if I had been holding *his* hand, we'd be a lot richer tonight!"

124. Three patients in a hospital ward were reprimanded severely for playing poker. As a final gesture, the nurse confiscated the deck of cards.

Later, one of the patients went down the floor and collected the medical charts from the beds. He returned, shuffled the charts, and dealt them out. "I've got a pair," he said, laying down two appendectomies.

"I've got that beat," replied the second patient, showing a full house—tonsillectomies over fractured legs.

The third patient chuckled softly. "It looks like I win," he said. "I've got a royal flush." He laid down his charts—five enemas.

125. An American tourist home from Formosa told how one night he decided to kill a little time playing poker with three wealthy Chinese. As he spoke no Chinese, and the almond-eyed brothers no English, they got an interpreter. All went quietly for a while, but in due course the American was dealt a four-card flush and bet a hundred dollars.

At this, the Chinese gentleman next to him exclaimed, "Ah moy," which the interpreter explained meant he raised a hundred. The next Chinese announced, "Ah foy," and the interpreter said, "He raises you two hundred more." The third Chinese grunted, "Ah goy," which the interpreter explained as another hundred raise.

In spite of the competition the American decided to stay with the pot, and drew his one card. Noting that he had failed to fill his flush, he cried, "Ah phooey," at which the Chinese all threw down their hands.

"Nice going, mister," cried the interpreter, slapping him on the back. "Your million dollar bluff won the pot."

Cause and effect

126. Two congressmen were lamenting the death of a colleague who had passed on the day before. "I understand," observed one, "that our friend T—— left very few effects."

"It would not be otherwise," replied his friend. "He had very few causes."

Chauvinism

127. An American staying in a London hotel was introduced to a man from Edinburgh who asked him, "An' what country do you belong tae?"

"The greatest country in the world!" replied the American.

"Mon! So dae I," replied Sandy, "but you dinna speak like a Scotsman."

128. An aged woman, born and nurtured in the South, was endeavoring to impress upon her nephews and nieces the beauties of the South and its people, when one of the young men spoke up.

"Auntie," he asked, "do you think that all of the virtues originated and have been preserved by the Southern people?"

"No, not all, but most of them," she replied.

"Do you think that Jesus Christ was a Southerner?" asked the young man.

The old lady hesitated a moment and then said: "He was good enough to be a Southerner!"

Child training

129. Never slap a child in the face. It is well to remember that there is a place for everything.

130. "My teenage son obeys me perfectly."

"Amazing. How do you do it?"

"I tell him to do as he pleases."

131. An elderly gentleman strolling through a quiet residential neighborhood came upon a little boy sitting on the curb crying copiously. "What's the trouble, son?" he asked. "Are you lost?"

"Worse than that," the youngster sobbed. "Mom's book on child-raising is lost, and now she's using her own judgment!"

Church affiliation

132. A businessman was interviewing a job applicant. "Now then," he stated briskly, "for this position we need a real live wire. But, at the same time, he must be methodical. I can't overemphasize the importance of his being methodical."

"Hm'm," the applicant said, after some thought, "if that's the case, I guess I don't want the job after all."

"No? Why not?"

"Well," replied the applicant, "it's that 'methodical.' All my life I've been a good Presbyterian, and I don't believe that I'm going to change now."

Church attendance

133. If men cared what other men wear, they'd be in church oftener.

134. If ever I build a church I will put this sign on every door: "You are not too bad to come in. You are not too good to stay out."

135. "Dad, can I ask you a question?"

"Sure, son."

"When am I going to be old enough not to have to go to church either?"

136. The two men were old friends. Said one, "I've been in the harness of the church for 22 years."

"Yes," said the other, "and during that time you've worn out 15 hold-back straps and only one collar."

137. A stranger stopping into an open church for a few minutes of contemplation found a purse in the pew in front of him. Since no one else was in the church, a question promptly rose in his mind: Was this a temptation of the Devil, or the answer to a prayer?

138. A man came home and saw his children on the front steps and asked what they were doing. "We're playing church," they answered.

The puzzled father inquired further and was told, "Well, we've already sung, prayed and preached, and now we're outside on the steps smoking."

139. In California, the Suisun-Fairfield Congregational Church bulletin published this item under the auspices of the pastor, the Rev. C. W. Kirkpatrick: "This . . . is . . . the . . . way . . . the . . . church . . . sometimes . . . looks . . . to . . . the . . . pastor . . . when . . . he . . . goes . . . into . . . the . . . pulpit.

"Wouldlooklikethisifeverybodybroughtsomebodyelseto church."

140. At a mental hospital in California one Sunday morning a group of patients were being shepherded to the Catholic and Protestant chapels. One patient did not enter either chapel, but continued walking toward the main gate. When an attendant caught up with him and asked where he was going the patient replied, "I was told I could go to the church of my choice, and that is in New York."

141. The little boy was late for Sunday school, and the superintendent, seeing him slip in, detained him and asked him the reason. The boy shuffled his feet uncertainly for a moment, then blurted out: "I started out to go fishing instead, but my dad wouldn't let me."

The superintendent beamed broadly. "A wise father," he said. "He was quite right not to let you go fishing on a Sunday. Did he explain to you why?"

The little boy nodded. "Oh, yes, sir. He said there wasn't enough bait for the two of us."

Church collections

142. "I've been racking my brains, but I can't place you," one man said to another at a gathering. "And you look very much like somebody I have seen a lot—somebody I don't like but I can't tell you why. Isn't that strange?"

"Nothing strange about it," the other man said. "You have seen me a lot and I know why you resent me. For two years I passed the collection plate in your church."

143. Little Mary was much surprised when she received a half dollar on her fifth birthday. She kept it in her hands constantly, and finally sat down on a stool, looking intently at the coin.

Her mother said, "Mary, what are you going to do with your half dollar?"

"I'll take it with me to Sunday school," said Mary promptly.

"I guess you want to show it to your teacher," suggested mother.

"Oh, no!" declared Mary. "I'm going to give it to God. I know He will be as surprised as I am to get something besides pennies!"

Citizenship

144. A Frenchman renounced his citizenship to become a British subject. "What have you gained by it?" demanded a countryman.

"Well," said the former Frenchman, "for one thing, I have now won the Battle of Waterloo."

145. A refugee couple arrived in the United States several years ago with one dream—to become citizens. Through much red tape and years of study, they were patient and hopeful. Then one day, the husband rushed into the kitchen with the long-awaited good news.

"Anna! Anna!" he shouted. "At last! We are Americans!"

"Fine," replied the wife, tying her apron around him. "Now you wash the dishes."

Civilization

146. An explorer came across a native village in the jungle. "You people are lost to civilization," he observed to the headman.

"We don't mind being lost," was the reply. "It's being discovered that worries us."

Class reunion. See Reunion, Class

Club membership

147. On being invited to join an actors' club, Groucho Marx remarked: "I wouldn't belong to any organization that would have me for a member."

148. "I've got too many organization dues to pay," Mrs. Hillis murmured over her checkbook. "One of these days somebody's going to read on my tombstone—'Christine Hillis. Clubbed to death.'"

149. "I am the recording secretary of a chess club," the man advised the judge who had asked him for his occupation.
"And what are your duties?"
"I read the hours of the last meeting."

Coexistence

150. Zoo visitors were amazed to see a cage, labeled "Coexistence," containing a lion and some lambs.
The zoo director explained there was nothing to it. "Just add a few fresh lambs every now and then."

College

151. The type of education a college person gets sometimes depends on the type of institution he attends—educational or coeducational.

152. Colleges and insane asylums both are mental institutions in a way. But one has to show some improvement to graduate from an asylum.

153. "The college I went to turned out some great men."
"When did you graduate?"
"I didn't exactly graduate. I was turned out."

154. *Friend:* "Has your son's college education proved helpful since you took him into the firm?"

Father: "Oh yes, whenever we have a conference, we let him mix the cocktails."

155. *Friend:* "You look all broken up."
College student: "I wrote home for money for a study lamp."
Friend: "So what?"
College student: "They sent the lamp."

156. "How come your son is doing so well in college?"
"Well, wine makes him sick, he's afraid of women, he hates to play games, he's allergic to the sun, and he can't sing, so he just stays home and studies."

Common cause

157. "Some years ago I was driving down Broadway with my sister. Suddenly she boomed out, 'Slow up. Slow up. Slow up.' I don't know why, but somehow women always say things three times.

"Just to show her who was driving the car, I said, 'Shut up,' and for emphasis pressed my foot on the accelerator. We really started to move down Broadway. But not for long.

"Out of nowhere came a gorilla on a motorcycle. A siren screeched—and a roar deafened my ears—'GET OVER THERE!' The car whimpered to the curb automatically.

"After what seemed eternity a huge head filled the whole window of the car.

"'What's the hurry?' he rasped.

"There didn't seem any hurry at that point—but just then my mother's favorite daughter howled, 'Give him a ticket, Officer. Give him a ticket. He's always speeding, always, always.'

"'Get out of that car, Bud,' panted the Gorilla.

"I walked to the rear of the car, thinking, 'I'll get thirty days for this one!'

"As I looked up at the towering policeman he leaned down over me and in the softest voice you ever heard whispered, *'Go on, Bud, I got one at home just like her."*

—DAVID GUY POWERS

Communism

158. A famous athlete, who had recently escaped from behind the Iron Curtain, was asked why the Russians excelled in marathon running.

He replied: "We use the border for the finish line."

159. A German and a Russian were fishing on opposite sides of the river. The German caught fish after fish, while the Russian didn't even get a bite. Finally the Russian yelled across, "Why is it you catch fish and I get none?"

The German thought a minute and then replied, "I guess on your side they are afraid to open their mouths."

160. Three cellmates in a Soviet hoosegow compared notes.

"I was jailed for coming late to work," mourned the first.

"Me? I came too early," recounted the second. "They said this proved I was a Capitalist spy."

"And I'm here," complained the third, "because I arrived exactly on time. They accused me of owning an American watch."

161. A French poodle met a Russian wolfhound on the Champs Elysees in Paris. "How are things in Russia?" asked the French poodle.

"Fabulous," the Russian wolfhound replied. "I sleep in a solid gold dog house on a sable carpet, and all day long they feed me caviar."

"Well," asked the French poodle, "if things are so good in Russia, why do you come to Paris?" The Russian wolfhound leaned forward. "Well," he whispered confidentially, "sometimes I like to bark."

162. A Moscow father was complimenting another on his three sons.

"You must be mighty proud of them," he said. "One a people's doctor, one a people's lawyer, and one a people's artist."

"Yes, they're fine boys," said the father, "but the son I'm really proud of is in America."

"Oh, he's an American?"

"Yes, indeed—he's unemployed and gets money from the government and if it weren't for the few dollars he sends home we'd starve."

163. A small Russian boy was asked by his teacher, "What is the size of the Communist Party?"

"About five feet two inches," he promptly replied.

"Idiot!" exploded the teacher. "I mean how many members does it have? How do you get five feet two inches?"

"Well," replied the boy, "my father is six feet tall and every night he puts his hand to his chin and says, 'I've *had* the Communist Party, up to here!'"

164. In a Warsaw schoolroom, little Janek was asked to give an example of a dependent clause.

"Our cat has a litter of ten kittens," he piped, "all of which are good Communists."

Teacher, delighted with his grasp of grammar and Party Line, urged him to do as well when the government inspector made his annual visit.

Next week, with the inspector sternly observing, teacher confidently called on Janek.

"Our cat has a litter of ten kittens," Janek piped, "all of which are good Western Democrats."

Teacher cried, "Why, Janek! That is not what you said a week ago."

"Yes," replied Janek very seriously, "but my kittens' eyes are open now."

165. There was a meeting in an iron curtain country at which one of the party members, Comrade Popsky, got up and said, "Comrade leader, I have only three questions to ask. If we are the greatest industrial nation in the world, what happened to our automobiles? If we have the best agriculture in the world, what happened to our bread? If we are the finest cattle raisers in the world, what happened to our meat?"

The presiding chairman stared at Comrade Popsky, hardly believing what he heard. Then he answered, "It is too late to reply to your questions tonight. At our next meeting I will answer them fully."

When the meeting opened the following week, another party member rose and said, "I have just one question. What happened to Comrade Popsky?"

Companionship

166. She's the kind of girl who doesn't care for a man's company—unless he owns it.

167. "Drink?"
"No."
"Neck?"
"No."
"Well, do you eat hay?"
"Of course not!"
"Gad, you're not fit company for man or beast."

Competition

168. A bunch of chickens was in the yard when a football flew over the fence and landed in their midst. A rooster waddled over, studied it, then said: "I'm not complaining, girls, but look at the work they're turning out next door."

169. A tourist traveling through the Southwest bought a buckskin and beaded trinket from an Indian for $3. The brave assured him it was authentic tribal craftsmanship. His squaw had learned the art from her great grandmother.

An hour later the tourist came back red-faced with anger. "There's a fellow on the other side of town selling these same things for a dollar," he shouted. "This shows you can't trust an Indian."

"No," replied the Indian unperturbed. "It shows you can't trust white man. Feller who sold me these promised no one else in town gettum."

Complaint—Complaints

170. One stormy night, Frank Lloyd Wright, noted Wisconsin architect, was roused from a sound sleep by an urgent phone call from a client who had just moved into his Wright-built house.

"There's a leak in the roof and the living room is flooded," cried the man. "What shall I do?"

Advised Wright, "Rise above it."

171. The desk clerk received a call from one of the hotel's guests, an old maid, who complained, "There's a man across the court taking a shower and he's got the blinds up."

The house detective was sent to the woman's room to investigate. He looked out her window and then said, "I can't see a man over there."

"You can't?" replied the old maid. "Get up on that trunk and look again."

Conceit

172. Sir Herbert Beerbohm Tree, British actor and manager, once berated a young actor for his overbearing conceit.

"I assure you, sir," said the other indignantly, "that I am not suffering from a swelled head."

"It isn't the swelling that causes suffering," retorted Tree. "It's the subsequent shrinkage that hurts."

Confusion

173. It seems to me that we're all in the same boat with Christopher Columbus. He didn't know where he was going when he started. When he got there he didn't know where he was, and when he got back he didn't know where he had been.

174. The biology club at the university was sponsored by one of the professors, a dignified spinster. A farmer, whose place was noted for its wide variety of flowers, spoke at one of the meetings.

More at home in his garden than as a speaker, he began by saying, "I can assure you that it is a pleasure for me to be with you today. I have known your teacher a good many years and during that time we have been intimate."

There was a slight titter and he hastily continued, "in a biological sense, of course."

Conscience

175. An eager-beaver salesman was trying to have a country storekeeper carry his product, and finally tried to bribe the fellow with a bottle of champagne.

"Oh, my conscience wouldn't let me take a gift," the merchant protested.

"What if I sell it to you for a dime?" asked the salesman.

"In that case," replied the merchant, "I'll take two."

Context, Out of

176. A sedate English literary man was interviewed by reporters on his arrival in New York. He remembered that he had been warned before leaving London that American newshawks would probably try to make a fool of him.

"Are you going to visit any night clubs during your stay in New York?" was the first question asked.

"Are there any night clubs in New York?" parried the literary man.

The next day he opened his morning paper to an account of the interview. According to the story, the first question he had asked on stepping ashore was: "Are there any night clubs in New York?"

Conversation

177. Three ways to break up a dinner conversation . . .

1. Ask the lady on your right if she is married. If she says yes, ask her if she has any children. If she says no, ask her how she does it.

2. Ask the lady on your left if she is married. If she says no, ask her if she has any children.

3. Lean across the table and ask the lady facing you if she has any children. If she says yes, ask her if she is married.

Cooking

178. "Jack, wake up. There's a burglar in the kitchen and he's eating up the rest of the pie we had for dinner."

"Go back to sleep. I'll bury him in the morning."

179. "I clipped this recipe from a magazine in the reading room of the library," said the housewife. "I suppose I did wrong."

Husband, surveying the dish: "You undoubtedly incurred the wrath of the librarians, but on the other hand, no one knows how many husbands ought to be eternally grateful."

180. It was baking day and the busy farm wife was being assisted by her ten-year-old daughter.

"Paula," she said, "open the oven and see if that coffee cake is baked. Just stick in a knife and see if it comes out clean."

Paula returned in a few minutes and said, "Mom, the knife came out so clean I stuck in all the other dirty knives."

181. A young bride had not come out very well in her first encounter with the cook book and gas stove. She ran to the telephone and called her mother.

"Mother," she sobbed, "I can't understand it. The recipe says clearly, 'bring to a boil on brisk fire, stirring for two minutes. Then beat it for ten minutes.' And when I came back again, it was burned to a cinder."

Cooperation

182. There is little chance for people to get together as long as most of us want to be in the front of the bus, the back of the church, and the middle of the road.

183. A very nice looking young lady walked into a sporting goods store and ordered all the equipment necessary for a baseball game including a baseball, a bat, a catcher's mitt, and a catcher's mask.

"Are you sure you want all these?" asked the salesman.

The girl answered, "Yes, I do. My boss said if I'd play ball with him we'd get along fine."

Courage

184. "I resent your remark," said the fifth grader. "And I'll give you just five seconds to take it back!"

"Oh, yeah," snarled the seventh grader. "Suppose I don't take it back in five seconds?"

"Well," said the first, "how much time do you want?"

185. Having missed his train to the suburbs a meek gentleman decided to fortify himself with a drink or two. Finding the liquor a great consolation he started back to the station, but lost his way. While groping about he happened to pass a zoo, and feeling sleepy, he opened the lion's cage and fell asleep with his head comfortably resting on the king of beasts' stomach.

The next day his wife set out to search for him and found him snoring blissfully in the middle of the lion's den. "Come out of there," she shrieked. "Come out, you little coward!"

186. When President Teddy Roosevelt was touring Oklahoma, he drove by to see his old friend, Quanah Parker, chief of the Comanches, who lived 12 miles from Fort Sill. With pride Parker showed Teddy the house he lived in, the white man's clothes he wore and his children who attended the white man's school.

"See here, Chief," Teddy said, "why don't you set your people a still better example of obeying the laws of the land and the customs of the whites? A white man has only one wife, and here you are living with five squaws. Why don't you give up four of them and remain faithful to the fifth? Then you would really be living as the white man lives."

Parker considered the proposition. "You are my great white father," he said, "and I will do as you wish on one condition."

"You pick out the one I am to live with—and then you go tell the other four."

Courtship. See also Romance

187. Courtship makes a man spoon but it's matrimony which makes him fork over.

188. *He:* "Have you ever loved before?"
She: "No, John. I've often admired men for their looks, strength, courage, intelligence, or something like that. But with you, John, it's love—nothing else."

189. "Do you truly love me?"
"Very much, indeed."
"Well, just how much?"
"Here's my check book. Just check the stubs."

Cowardice

190. "I'd like to make an appointment with the dentist please."
"Sorry, he's out just now."
"When will he be out again?"

191. Former Governor Jack Walton of Oklahoma disposed of a tough opponent with this gem of political destruction: "My opponent brags that he is a hard-boiled egg! Well, folks, I never saw a hard-boiled egg that didn't have a yellow heart!"

Credit

192. "Do you live within your income?"
"Certainly not. I have all I can do to live within my credit."

193. An elderly farmer wrote to a mail order house as follows: "Please send me one of the gasoline engines you show on page 787, and if it's any good, I'll send you a check."

In time he received the following reply: "Please send check. If it's any good, we'll send the engine."

194. When a familiar face was missing from the regular get-togethers the wife of one of the clique called to inquire the reason.

"You might as well know the truth," the man's wife said. "I put so much pressure on Bob to keep up appearances that he went out and got two years for stealing a Cadillac."

When Bob was paroled a few months later the couple found themselves ostracized by their old crowd; the woman who had called explained the reason.

"We can't mingle with criminals," she said bluntly. "Why did you have to steal a Cadillac? Couldn't you buy one and not pay for it, like the rest of us?"

Credulity

195. A group of foreign manufacturers, who were being shown through an American plant, saw a machine that took a piece of sheet steel and in one operation stamped, punched, and shaped it into a finished product. After they had watched it for a time, an apparently bitter argument broke out among them, with much arm-waving and finger-shaking. The guide asked the interpreter accompanying the party what all the shouting was about.

"Some of them," replied the interpreter nonchalantly, "insist it can't be done!"

Crime—Punishment

196. A teacher asked the class to name some of the benefits of the automotive age. After a silence, one boy spoke up, "Well, it stopped horse stealing."

197. "How long are you in jail for, Jim?"
"Two weeks."
"What's the charge?"
"No charge, everything is free."
"I mean, what did you do?"
"Oh, I shot my wife."
"You killed your wife and only in jail for two weeks?"
"That's all—then I get hanged."

Criticism

198. It's better to help others get on than to tell them where to get off.

199. Heywood Broun, the New York newspaperman, was leaving the theater after a Broadway opening and met the producer in the lobby. The latter took one look at Broun's suit, which was rumpled as usual, and said with some annoyance:

"That's a fine way to dress for my opening. Your suit looks as if it had been slept in."

"Since you mention it," replied Broun, "I just woke up."

D

Dancing

200. *Night club patron* (approvingly watching a gorgeous Latin go through her torrid dance routine): "Lots of pepper!"
Friend: "Nice shaker, too!"

201. It happened in a teenage rock-n-roll joint. The waiter dropped a tray of dishes and six couples got up to dance.

202. A man who was a stranger in town was taken to a dance at a deaf and dumb hospital by a doctor friend of his.

"But how on earth can I ask a deaf and dumb girl to dance?" he asked.

"Just smile and bow to her," explained the doctor, who had done it before.

So the young man picked out a pretty girl, smiled and bowed to her, and away they danced. They danced not only one dance but three, and he was on the point of asking her for another dance when a strange man approached his fair partner and said lovingly: "Darling, when are we going to have another dance? It's been over an hour since I danced with you."

"I don't know, dear," said the girl tenderly. "I don't know how to get away from this deaf and dumb idiot!"

Debt

203. *Ted:* "I started out on the theory that the world had an opening for me."

Fred: "And you found it?"

Ted: "Well, kinda, I'm in the hole now."

204. *Sympathizer:* "Tell me, friend, how did you ever get yourself into such destitute circumstances?"

Derelict: "Well, when I had the world by the tail, I let go to reach for the moon."

Debtor—Creditor

205. Running into debt isn't so bad. It's running into creditors that hurts.

206. The installment collector came around to remind Joe he was seven payments behind on his piano. "Well," replied Joe, "the company advertises 'pay as you play'—and I play very poorly."

207. "I don't see why you haggled so with the tailor about the price—you'll never pay his bill, anyhow," said Pat to Mike.

"Yes, but, you see, I'm conscientious. I don't want the poor fellow to lose more than is necessary."

208. The butcher confronted the customer with embarrassment. "I'm sorry, madam, but I can't give you further credit. Your bill is bigger now than it should be."

"I'm aware of that," the woman exclaimed. "If you'll make it out for what it should be, I'll pay it."

209. "Will you tell me, my dear friend, how you manage, that you are never pressed for money, but always have plenty of it?"

"That is very simple; I never pay old debts."

"But how about the new ones?"

"I let them grow old."

210. A taxpayer received a strongly worded "second notice" that his taxes were overdue. Hastening to the collector's office, he paid his bill, saying apologetically that he had overlooked the first notice.

"Oh," confided the collector with a smile, "we don't send out first notices. We have found that the second notices are more effective."

211. A merchant tried for many months to collect an overdue bill, but with no success. Finally, he sent a tear-jerking letter accompanied by a picture of his little daughter. Under it he wrote, "The reason I need the money."

By return mail came a photo of a voluptuous blonde in a bikini bathing suit. It was captioned, "The reason I can't pay."

212. A man called a dozen of his creditors to tell them that he was about to go into bankruptcy.

"I owe you over $100,000," he said, "and my assets aren't enough to pay you five cents on the dollar. So I guess it will be impossible for you to get anything—unless you want to cut me up and divide me among you."

"Say, Mr. Chairman," spoke up one creditor, "I move we do it. I'd like to have his gall."

213. In one of those western scenes so familiar on TV, two groups of men were shooting it out in the barroom of a shabby roadhouse.

Suddenly a meek little man entered the door and started right across the room toward the bar. All the shooting stopped.

The bartender got up from behind the safety of the bar and said, "Partner, it sure took real courage to walk right through all those six guns without lookin' right nor left."

"Not at all," replied the meek little man as he asked for a sarsaparilla. "You see, I owe money to every one in the place."

Deception

214. Two little fellows coming home from Sunday school were discussing the lesson.

"Say, do you believe all that about the devil?"

"No, don't let them kid you. That's just like Santa Claus— it's your old man."

Democracy

215. The hydrogen bomb has made one great contribution to democracy. With it—all men are cremated equal.

Destination

216. The average man's life consists of twenty years of having his mother ask him where he is going; forty years of having his wife ask the same question; and at the end, the mourners wondering, too.

217. A man "butted in" at a waiting line before the ticket window in New York and the men who were in a hurry glowered.

"I want a ticket for Boston," said the man, and he put fifty cents under the wicket.

"You can't go to Boston for fifty cents," returned the ticket agent.

"Well, then," asked the man, "where can I go for fifty cents?"

And each of the fourteen men in that waiting line quickly told him!

Diagnosis

218. "Doctor, what is wrong with me?"

"Madame, you are too fat, you use too much rouge and lipstick, you get your hair bleached, you smoke too much and one other thing—you are in the wrong office. The doctor is next door. I am nothing but a newspaper man."

219. The middle-aged man was shuffling along, bent over at the waist, as his wife helped him into the doctor's waiting room. A woman in the office viewed the scene in sympathy. "Arthritis with complications?" she asked.

The wife shook her head. "Do-it-yourself," she explained, "with concrete blocks."

220. Being human, doctors are reluctant to make house calls where receipt of payment is doubtful. Under these circumstances a physician diagnosed a patient's illness on the phone. "There is nothing wrong with your uncle. I have examined him thoroughly and I tell you he only thinks he's sick. He thinks he's sick."

A week later the doctor met the patient's nephew. "How's your uncle?" he asked.

"Worse," said the relative. "Now he thinks he's dead."

Diet—Dieting

221. Diets are for people who are thick and tired of it.

222. Seating his dinner guests, a doctor asked, "Are we going to eat like men or beasts?" The somewhat shocked guests replied: "Like men, of course."

"Oh, that's too bad," said the doctor, "because beasts would stop eating when they got enough."

223. Methuselah ate what he found on his plate,
And never, as people do now,
Did he note the amount of the calorie count;
He ate it because it was chow.

He wasn't disturbed as at dinner he sat,
Devouring a roast or a pie,
To think it was lacking in granular fat
Or a couple of vitamins shy.

He cheerfully chewed each species of food,
Unmindful of troubles or fears
Lest his health might be hurt
By some fancy dessert;
And he lived over 900 years.
—Author unknown

Difference—Differences

224.   The difference between a mistress and a wife is the difference between day and night.

225.   A celebrated judge and an almost equally celebrated bishop were engaged in friendly argument as to which of them had more power over their fellow men. Explained the bishop: "After all, old man, you can only say to a man, 'You be hanged!' I can go very much further. I can say to a man, 'You be damned!'"

The judge nodded, smilingly. "Ah, yes," he said. "But the difference is that when I say to a man 'You be hanged!'—he *is* hanged."

226.   Adolf Hitler was very much disturbed when a clairvoyant let it be known that she could predict the exact day of the Fuhrer's death. Since her predictions were always based on

astrology, and since Hitler himself was a believer in the stars, he sent for the woman. After much divination the woman finally said that the omens indicated no specific date for the passing of the Nazi leader, other than that it would definitely take place on a Jewish holiday.

"Which holiday?" Hitler demanded.

"I cannot be sure," said the astrologist.

"You've got to be sure," Hitler ordered, going off into one of his spastic shrieks. "I demand that you be sure."

"What difference does it make?" shrugged the woman. "Any day on which you die will be a Jewish holiday."

Direction—Directions

227. At a New England dog show, two elderly matrons, after looking over the various breeds asked a young attendant, "Can you direct us to the Labradors?"

"Yes ma'am," replied the boy. "Straight down this aisle, and the second door on the left."

228. An old lady kept asking the bus driver to tell her when they arrived at a certain small town. She asked so often that finally the driver got nervous and passed through the small town before he realized it. He apologized to the other passengers, turned around, and drove back. Then he said to the old lady: "This is the town where you wanted to get out."

"Who wants to get out?" she answered.

The driver said: "You did."

"No," she said, "my daughter told me that when I pass through this town, I should take my pills."

229. During World War I, the London clubs extended courtesies to officers of Dominion Forces, much to the annoyance of the retired field officers who were accustomed to preempt the leather armchairs in the club library. One afternoon, a colonial officer, slightly the worse for cocktails, entered the library, tapped a grumpy old general on the shoulder and asked a question using very vulgar language.

The general dropped his newspaper, screwed his monocle in his eye and looked the colonial up and down and said, "Go out that door, turn left till you come to a corridor. Follow the corridor until you come to a sign marked *gentlemen* . . . but don't let that deter you!"

Disappointment

230. *Young lady:* "Officer, a sailor came into my cabin last night."

Officer: "What do you expect in Second Class, lady, the Captain?"

231. The minister of a church discovered at the last minute that he hadn't invited a little old lady congregant to come to his garden party and called her up and asked her to come out.

"It's no use," she informed him. "I've already prayed for rain."

232. His team was behind one run in the ninth inning, two were out and the bases were loaded. He was the leading hitter on the team. The crowd sat on the edge of its seat as he swung two bats, threw away one, picked up the rosin bag, dropped it, straightened his cap, knocked the dirt from his spikes, wiped his brow, raised the bat over his shoulder and wiggled it, pounded it on the plate, straightened his cap once more, pulled up his pants, dug his spikes in, cocked his bat over his shoulder, reached forward—and then watched the pitcher pick the runner off third base.

Divorce

233. *Lawyer:* "Why do you want a divorce?"

Disgruntled wife: "Because we have nothing in common. Why, we don't even hate the same people."

234. *Disillusioned wife:* "I'd like to get a divorce. My husband and I just don't get along."

Friend: "Why don't you sue on the grounds of incompatibility."

Wife: "I would if I could catch him at it."

235. A couple whose marriage was going on the rocks sought the advice of a marriage counsellor.

The counsellor pleaded with them to patch up their quarrel, but they were adamant. "So," said the counsellor, "you know the consequences and you want to part. Remember this. You must divide your property equally."

The wife flared up. "You mean the $4,000 I have saved up? I must give him half? My money?"

"Yes," said the counsellor. "He gets $2,000. You get $2,000."

"What about my furniture? I paid for that."

"Same thing," answered the counsellor. "Your husband gets the bedroom and the living room; you get the dining room and the kitchen."

There was a challenging gleam in the wife's eye. "What about our three children?"

That stumped him. Shrewdly he assayed the situation, then he came up with a Solomonic answer. "Go back and live together until your fourth child is born. Then you take two children and your husband takes two."

The wife shook her head. "No, I'm sure that wouldn't work out. If I depended on him, I wouldn't have the three I got."

Doctor—Patient

236. There's another advantage in being poor. The doctor will cure you faster.

237. "His doctor told him he was in as good shape as a man of 60, but the trouble was he was only 45."

238. "Oh, doctor," said the young lady, "will the scar show?"

"That, madam," said the doctor, "is entirely up to you."

239. *Doctor:* "Well, you are coughing with less exertion today!"

Patient: "That's not surprising, doctor, since I practiced that all night."

240. Gazing fondly at his attractive nurse, the hospital patient told the doctor. "Wonderful nurse you've got here. One touch of her hand cooled my fever instantly."

"I know," answered the doctor, "I could hear her slap clear to the end of the corridor."

241. The surgeon was discussing a forthcoming operation with a wealthy patient.

"Would you prefer a local anaesthetic?" he inquired.

"I can afford the best," replied the wealthy patient. "Get something imported."

242. A town doctor was in bed when his phone rang and an excited voice told him that the baby had swallowed a corkscrew. The doctor was about to leave for the address that was given to him when his phone rang again.

The same voice on the line said: "It's all right now, doctor. We've found another corkscrew."

243. A hillbilly was making his first visit to a hospital where his teenage son was about to have an operation. Watching the doctor's every move, he asked, "What's that?"

The doctor explained, "This is an anaesthetic; after he gets this he won't know a thing."

"Save your time, Doc," exclaimed the man, "he don't know anything now."

244. A contractor was hosting his friends at an open house affair to celebrate the opening of a new shop and showroom.

"If my doctor could see me with this champagne and caviar, he'd go crazy," the host confided to a friend.

"Why?" asked the buddy. "You supposed to be on a diet?"

"Naw," replied the contractor. "I owe him $300."

245. A fellow consulted a doctor because he wasn't feeling well.

"Do you smoke excessively?" asked the M.D.

"No."

"Drink a lot?"

"No."

"Keep late hours?"

"Nope."

The doctor shook his head and asked, "How can I cure you if you have nothing to give up?"

246. Just after Pete was admitted to the hospital, he heard a knock at the door of his room. "Come in," Pete said, and in came a woman. "I'm your doctor," she said. "Please take off your clothes."

Pete asked her if she meant for him to remove all of his clothing and she told him that was just what she did mean. So he took off all his clothes and she examined him: nose, throat, chest, stomach, thighs, feet. When she finished her examination she announced: "You may get into bed. Do you have any questions?"

"Just one," said Pete. "Why did you knock?"

247. A friend of mine was going around town, his mouth open, gasping for breath, his eyes popping out. So he went to the doctor, and the doctor told him he had only three months to live. He decided therefore to spend all his money. He bought everything he could think of. Then one day he ambled into a haberdashery shop and said, "Give me a dozen shirts, size 14½ in the neck, 32 in the sleeves."

"Wait a minute," said the salesman, "you'd better let me measure your neck." He threw a tape measure around my friend's neck.

"You need a size 16," he announced. "If you took a 14½, you'd be going around all the time with your mouth open, gasping for breath, your eyes popping out."

248. Thoroughly steeped in ethics, a physician always insisted on the presence of a third party in the room whenever he examined a female patient.

Near the close of a busy afternoon, he wearily motioned a couple into the examining room. The woman complained of pains in her lower abdomen, and submitted to examination reluctantly. The man looked on with unfeigned interest.

When he had finished, the doctor prescribed some medicine, and the woman jumped up from the table, dressed hurriedly, and ran out of the room.

"Your wife's certainly lively," commented the doctor. "She'll be all right in a few days."

"My *wife?*" said the man. "I never saw her before, Doc. I was wondering why you called me in here with you."

249. It was 3 o'clock on a cold, rainy morning when the doctor was awakened by an emergency phone call. Struggling out of bed, he pulled on his clothes, went out to his car, and finally got it started.

The patient lived miles across town, and it took the haggard doctor nearly an hour to get there, sliding sideways over the ice most of the way. When at last he arrived and examined the girl who was ill, he discovered she had nothing more than a severe cold.

"Why didn't you call me in the daytime?" the doctor inquired.

"We're poor people, sir, and not able to pay much," the father explained, "so we thought we'd call when you weren't too busy."

Do-it-yourself

250. One of these days somebody's going to come up with a book on "How to Get Out of Doing it Yourself." He'll make a fortune.

Doubt—Doubts

251. Following a knock on the door of an undergraduate's room at a university, a voice asked: "May I come in? This is the room I had when I was at college." He was invited in.

"Yes," he went on musingly. "Same old room. Same old furniture. Same old view from the window. Same old closet."

He opened the closet door. There stood a girl, looking scared.

"That is my sister," said the present occupant of the room.

"Yes," replied the visitor. "Same old story."

Dream—Dreams—Dreaming

252. Two fellows were discussing their dreams, and one said to the other: "Sam, did I ever dream last night—what a dream! I went to Coney Island, went on the chute-the-chute, had frankfurters and popcorn, took in all the side shows—it was the greatest dream in the world."

The other fellow said, "You're kidding. That's a dream? I had a much better one last night. I dreamed I went to a party, and I had Kim Novak on one arm and Jayne Mansfield on the other."

The first fellow said, "Gee, why didn't you call me?"

"I did," replied the other, "but your wife said you had gone to Coney Island."

Drinking

253. *Little girl:* "Mama! Daddy and I stopped on my way home. I had a coke and daddy had a glass of water with an olive in it."

254. After months at sea, the sailor hit port and headed for the nearest tavern. Pointing to a patron who lay prone on the floor, he instructed the barkeep, "Give me a shot of that."

255. In an Ohioan city there is a tavern called "The Office." Should one stop in after work and find he'll be late getting home he can truthfully call up and tell his wife that he's been delayed at the office.

256. Two bar pals met after not having seen each other for a long time. "My goodness," said one. "You have a funny color."

"Yah," replied the second. "I'm just getting over a rare disease. It's called 'Pistachio'; first you turn green and then you turn nuts."

257. Chauncey Depew told the story of a temperance lecturer who was caught by a disciple as he was downing a hot whiskey punch. "I thought you were a total abstainer," said the shocked fellow.

"I am," said the lecturer. "But I'm not a bigoted one."

258. Two lumbermen were drinking together at a bar when suddenly one lurched backward off his stool and lay flat on the floor without moving a muscle.

"One thing about Tom," said the other to the bartender, "he knows when to stop."

259. A young bride of three months complained to her mother about her husband's continued drinking habits.

"If you knew he drank, why did you marry him?" she was asked.

"I didn't know he drank," the girl replied, "until one night he came home sober!"

260. It was at an important local dance that Mrs. Brown found it necessary to protest to Mr. Brown.

"Do you know," she said, "you've been to the bar six times this evening?"

"That's all right, my dear," he replied. "I tell everybody I'm getting something for you."

261. "Why do you beg?"

"The truth is I beg to get money for booze."

"Why do you drink?"

"To give me the courage to beg."

262. Toulouse-Lautrec, the French painter, was a heavy drinker who always had a bottle handy.

On one occasion, a friend berated him for his drunkenness.

"How can you drink so much?" he demanded.

"I do not drink so much," replied the artist. "I only drink very little—very often."

263. Two waiters were standing at a table over which a loaded customer had fallen asleep. Said one:

"I've already awakened him twice. Now I'm going to awaken him for the third time."

"Why don't you throw him out?" asked the other waiter.

"The devil I will," said the first waiter. "I got a good thing going for me. Every time I wake him up he pays his bill."

264. The preacher was having a heart-to-heart talk with a backslider of his flock, whose drinking of moonshine invariably led to quarreling with his neighbors, and occasional shotgun blasts at some of them.

"Can't you see, Ben," intoned the parson, "that not one good thing comes out of this drinking?"

"Well, I sort of disagree there," replied the backslider. "It makes me miss the folks I shoot at."

265. A shipping clerk went to his doctor and complained of a pain in his leg. After one glance at the leg the doctor asked the patient: "How long have you been walking around in this condition?"

Clerk: "Two weeks."

Doctor: "For heaven's sake young man, you have a broken leg! Why didn't you come to me sooner?"

Clerk: "Well, doc, I would have, but every time I say something is wrong with me my wife says I have to give up drinking."

266. A well-dressed man came into the cocktail lounge each evening. He would be alone but always ordered two martinis. First he would drink one, then move over and drink the other.

The bartender's curiosity got the best of him, so one evening he asked the reason why two cocktails. The man explained that one was his and the other for his "best friend" who went west for his health. Then a few weeks later the man came in as usual but ordered only one martini. The bartender very solemnly asked, "What . . . only one? Did your friend pass away?"

The man replied, "Oh! No! I'm on the wagon."

267. There were numerous rumors that General Grant drank too much, and a delegation of Congressmen was appointed to find out the truth.

"Is it true," they asked him, "that you drink to excess?"

"To *what?*" asked Grant.

"To excess," said the leader of the delegation.

"Well, why not?" said Grant. "I just happen to have a bottle around, and if you don't mind taking it 'neat', let's all have a pull at it. Gentlemen—to excess!"

Drug store

268. *Customer:* "Give me some of that prepared mono-aceticacidester of salicylicacid."
Druggist: "Do you mean aspirin?"
Customer: "Yeah! I never can think of that name."

269. A man with a worried look on his face ran into a drug store and asked the druggist if he knew a way to stop the hiccoughs. Without any warning the druggist slapped him in the face. Amazed and angry, the young man demanded that the druggist explain his unusual behavior.

"Well," said the druggist, "you don't have the hiccoughs now do you?"

"No," answered the young man, "but my wife out in the car still does."

270. The drug store in a small town was closed down by its creditors. As he left the premises for the last time, the saddened proprietor paused long enough to tack this sign on the front door:

"Our doors are locked. The following services, formerly available here, may be had elsewhere from now on: *Ice-water* at fountain in the park. *General information* from the constable at the corner. *Change of a dollar* at the bank. *Matches and scratch pads* at the hotel. *Magazines for browsing* from the doctor. *Bus information* at the terminals. And *loafing* at any other location of your own choosing."

Drunkenness. See also Drinking

271. "Well, you can't say I made any noise coming in last night."

"No, but the men who were carrying you did."

272. "Who is the best lawyer in town?"

"Ferris Brown when he is sober."

"And who is the second best lawyer in town?"

"Ferris Brown when he is drunk."

273. "Why are you crying, little man?" said the old gent to a small boy.

"Father thrashed me for doing a crossword puzzle."

"Good gracious! Why?"

"Well, sir, one clue was a word of three letters meaning what is drunk every night—and I put *'dad'*!"

274. A college professor was invited to the Dean's house for cocktails. Later, realizing that he had exceeded his normal capacity, the prof was determined that no one should be aware of his indiscretion. As the party neared its conclusion, the wife of the Dean decided to show the latest addition to her family, and presently a nurse appeared carrying a bassinet containing twins. The prof looked into the bassinet and, trying to sound as normal as possible, said: "My, what a beautiful baby."

Education

275. "Say, Dad, did you go to Sunday school when you were a little boy?"

"Yes, son, regularly."

"Well, I'll bet it won't do me any good either."

276. "Yes, stamp collecting is educational," said the fond mother to the visitor. "For instance, where is Hungary, Eric?"

Without looking up from his stamp book, the young philatelist answered promptly: "Two pages in front of Italy."

277. *Father:* "I'm worried about your being at the bottom of the class."

Son: "Don't worry, Dad, they teach the same stuff at both ends."

Employer—Employee

278. Pity your boss. The poor guy has to get up early to see who comes in late.

279. If there were more self-starters, the boss wouldn't have to be a crank.

280. If at first you don't succeed, you're probably not related to the boss.

281. Is there anything so embarrassing as watching the boss doing something you told him couldn't be done?

282. When a secretary says the office staff is having a picnic, it may just mean that the boss is on vacation.

283. *Boss:* "This is just a suggestion. You don't have to follow it unless you want to keep your jobs."

284. "Have you an opening for a genius?"
"Yes, and don't slam the door on the way out."

285. "Miss Jones," said the baffled office manager, "how do you do it? You've been here two weeks, and you're already one month behind!"

286. *Interviewer:* "Young man, do you think you can handle a variety of work?"
Job hunter: "I ought to be able to. I've had 12 different jobs in less than six months."

287. The boss was pointing out to his secretary several errors she had made during the day, when she interrupted with, "Mr. Jones, it's two minutes past five and you're annoying me on my own time."

288. "Do you believe in life after death?" an employer asked the office boy.
"Oh, yes, sir," was the reply.
"Ah, then everything is in order, because after you had gone to your grandfather's funeral yesterday, he came here to see you."

289. Then there was the dejected employee who came home one evening and slumped into a chair.

"Well," he said resignedly, "the worst has happened."

"Why, whatever happened, dear?" his wife asked anxiously.

"The boss called me in at quitting time and gave me the business."

290. A young man, tired of working for others, went into business for himself. Later a friend asked him how it was to be his own boss.

"I don't know," he replied. "The police won't let me park in front of my own place of business; tax collectors tell me how to keep books; my banker tells me how much balance I must maintain; freight agents tell me how my goods must be packed; customers tell me how my goods must be made; federal, state, county and local agencies tell me how to keep records; the union tells me whom I can employ and how and when; and on top of that, I just got married."

291. During the noontime recreational activities the president of the corporation mounted the platform, accompanied by an overall-clad man off the assembly line, and made this speech:

"Ladies and gentlemen, you are about to see how American industry rewards those who are conscientious and hard-working. This man standing beside me has been with the company less than a year, during which time his unusual qualities have earned him salary increases in excess of one hundred dollars a week. I have watched him closely, observed with great pleasure the manner in which he has pitched in and gotten things done. Therefore, I am pleased to announce that starting this very afternoon he gets out of his work clothes, comes into the executive branch, and takes over an office with the title of Executive Vice President in Charge of Policy at an annual wage of eighty thousand dollars. Congratulations to you, sir."

The workman shook the extended hand and said: "Gee, thanks, Dad."

Employment

292. For this job we want someone who is responsible.
"That's for me. Everywhere I've worked, whenever something went wrong, I was responsible."

293. *Shopper:* "Why, Mr. Smith, you are back again as floor walker! I thought you were now an insurance man."
Smith: "You made the same mistake I did."

294. "Do I detect the odor of liquor on your breath?" a stingy boss asked his sales manager.
"You do," admitted the sales manager. "I've just been celebrating the twentieth anniversary of the last raise you gave me."

295. On the job application blank was the question, "Have you ever been arrested?" The applicant put down, "No."
The next question was "Why"—meant for those who had been arrested. Not realizing this, the applicant put down, "Never been caught."

296. A secretary was applying for a new job. Under "office experience" on the application blank she wrote: "I'm familiar with all the important phases of office procedure—including bowling, crossword puzzles, coffee breaks, personal letter-writing and collection-taking."

297. "What does your husband do?" one wife asked another.
"He's an expediter."
"What's that?"
"Well, it's hard to explain but if we women did what he does, they'd call it nagging."

298. The president called in eight of his department heads for confidential discussion. "I understand," he said, "that all of you have been dating Miss Jones, the receptionist. I want the truth now. How many of you have been taking her out?"

Seven of the executives raised their hands and looked sheepish. The big boss glared at the eighth man and intoned: "Are you *sure* that you are telling the truth?"

"Yes, I am," was the reply.

"All right then," came the punchline. "*You* fire her."

299. The Smithsons went away for their summer vacation and gave their maid, Jane, a month's wages before leaving. On their return four weeks later, Jane demanded higher wages, or she would leave.

Mrs. Smithson was horrified. "Gracious," she exclaimed, "you've only just had a month off with full pay. You should consider yourself very fortunate."

"That's just it," she replied. "You paid me all that money for doing nothing, so how can you expect me to do all this work now for the same wages?"

300. The story is told of the owner of a large department store who went over his books and discovered that his most trusted employee had stolen over a million dollars from the firm.

"I want no scandal," the owner said. "I'll just fire you and forget about the entire matter."

The employee replied, "So you're going to fire me. True, I robbed your concern of quite a tidy sum. I now have yachts, a country mansion, a town house, jewelry, and every luxury you can think of. I don't need a thing, so why hire somebody else and have him start from scratch?"

301. A man applying for a job asked the interviewer whether the company would pay for his hospital insurance. The interviewer said the worker would have to pay for it but it was deducted from his check.

"The last place I worked the company paid for it," he said.

"Did they pay for your life insurance too?" the interviewer asked.

"Sure they did," the man said. "Not only that, but we got unlimited sick leave, severance pay, three weeks' vacation, a Christmas bonus, coffee breaks . . ."

"Then why did you leave such a perfect place?" the interviewer asked.

"The company folded," the man replied.

302.　A man knocked at the heavenly gate,
　　　　His face was scarred and old.
　　　He stood before the Man of Fate
　　　　For admission to the fold.
　　　"What have you done," St. Peter asked,
　　　　"To gain admission here?"
　　　"I've been an executive, Sir," he said,
　　　　"For many and many a year."
　　　The pearly gates swung open wide;
　　　　St. Peter touched the bell.
　　　"Come in and choose your harp," he said,
　　　　"You've had your share of hell."
　　　　　　　　　　　　—Author unknown

Epitaph—Epitaphs

303.　Occasionally, professional men have taken as their epitaphs phrases from their earthly work.

One doctor, for example, finally flouted the rule that prohibits physicians from advertising. He had the following carved on his headstone: *"Office Upstairs."*

Not to be outdone, a lawyer's gravestone read: *"Final Decree."*

And a henpecked barrister simply listed the names of his three wives, then proclaimed: *"The Defense Rests."*

Evolution

304. Man, in his anxiety to refute evidence that he is a monkey, manages to further the belief that he is an ass.

305. Somebody must take a chance. The monkeys who did became men, and the monkeys who didn't are still jumping around in trees making faces at the monkeys who did.

Excuse—Excuses

306. When the Moors were at the height of their cultural development this story was told about them. A Moorish farmer called at the home of his neighbor and asked if he might borrow a rope. "Oh, good and faithful neighbor, I must regretfully refuse of you this simple favor," spoke the man. "The rope you request cannot be given, for I use it to tie up my milk."

"But surely," replied the would-be borrower, "milk cannot be tied up with a rope?"

"By Allah," the refuser said. "When one does not want to do a thing, one reason is as good as another."

Expert—Experts

307. The fellow had spent his entire life studying goldfish. At a meeting of the Goldfish Lovers of America he was asked how one could tell the difference between a male goldfish and female goldfish.

"That's simple," said the man of knowledge. "Male goldfish will eat only male worms."

"But how," persisted the questioner, "can you tell the difference between male worms and female worms?"

"Haven't the slightest idea," he replied. "I'm not an expert on worms . . . just goldfish."

308. A kind-hearted motorist saw a man struggling to change a tire alongside the highway. There was a dirty smear across his red face where he had wiped off the sweat with dirty hands. His tie was undone, his shirt collar askew, and obviously he had also wiped his hands on his once-white shirt. Close to him stood a slight woman, immaculately neat, and arguing angrily.

"Look, friend," said the kind-hearted motorist. "I've changed a lot of tires. Is there anything I can do to help?"

"There sure is," replied the man with the tire tool. "My wife is an expert, too. If you will just do all the arguing with her about how this tire ought to be changed, I can concentrate on the dirty work and get the job done."

Failure

309. The tramps sat with their backs against an oak tree. Before them was a rippling stream. Although the day was delightful, one of them was disconsolate.

"You know, Jim," he mused, "this business of tramping your way through life is not what it's cracked up to be. Think it over—nights on park benches or in a cold barn. Traveling on freight trains and always dodging the police. Being kicked from one town to another. Wondering where your next meal is coming from. Wandering, unwanted everywhere, sneered at by your fellow men." His voice trailed off as he sighed heavily. His companion shifted his position slightly.

"Well," observed the second tramp, "if that's the way you feel about it, why don't you go and find yourself a job?"

The first tramp sat up with a jerk, opening his mouth in amazement. "What?" he exclaimed. "And admit I'm a failure?"

Fair play

310. One day, about six score years ago, two young fellows were in a quarrel, and it had signs of becoming serious. Abraham Lincoln, himself a young man but with an earnest desire for fair play, was called upon to decide the difficulty. One of the combatants, who had been defeated in the decision, and above whom the towering Lincoln stood head and shoulders, boastfully threatened Lincoln.

"See here, Lanky, I'll lick you!" he shouted.

Abe looked down comically at the small challenger. "All right," he said, "but let's fight fair. You are so small there isn't much of you for me to hit, but I am so big, you can't help hitting me. So you make a chalkmark on me that will show just your size. When we fight, you must be sure to hit me inside this mark or it won't be fair."

The idea was so ridiculous, the little bully began to laugh, and the quarrel ended as a joke.

Fame

311. An old man living in an apartment with his grandson heard that Jascha Heifetz had moved next door. He was so overcome with emotion at the news that he ran into Heifetz's apartment and said, "Oh, Mr. Heifetz, to think that such a great man as yourself is living next door to me. I can't believe it! My grandson will be overjoyed—he worships you."

Heifetz, wanting to be a good neighbor, offered to play his violin for the grandson, whereupon the old man said, "Oh—you play the fiddle, too?"

312. "What's your name?" asked the store manager of the young boy who was applying for a job.

"Ford," replied the lad.

"And your first name?"

"Henry."

"Henry Ford, eh?" queried the manager with a smile. "That's a pretty well known name."

The boy looked pleased. "Yes, sir, it should be," he replied proudly. "I've been delivering groceries around town for two years now."

313. A small boy went with his family for a visit of several days in New York City and of all the sights they saw his big favorite was the majestic statue of General Sherman on horseback at Fifth Avenue and 59th Street.

He asked to be taken back to the statue several times and, every time he went, he asked countless questions about the great Northern general. On the trip back to his home he was still cross-examining his father on the details of Sherman's deeds in the Civil War.

"But, Daddy, there's one thing I don't understand," he said finally. "Who is that man who was sitting on General Sherman?"

Familiarity

314. An editor, weary of the abuse following his editorials, ran the Ten Commandments in his editorial column.

A few days later came a letter: "Cancel my subscription. You're getting too personal."

315. The doctor had been called to look over Grandma, who had been complaining of aches and pains. He gave her a thorough going-over.

After he left, Grandma seemed to perk up a bit. "What did you say was the name of that new minister?" she asked.

"That wasn't the minister—that was the doctor," she was told.

"Hmmm, I thought he was a bit familiar for a minister," Grandma replied.

Family

316. A fellow we know was the youngest of 14 children. He was 20 years old before he found there were other parts of a chicken besides the gravy.

317. *Pompous speaker:* "There are 100 jails in this state and I'm proud to say that no members of my family have ever been in one of them."

Voice from the rear: "And which one is that?"

318. *Customer:* "I want an alarm clock that will wake father without arousing the whole family."

Clerk: "We have only the ordinary kind that will awaken the entire family without disturbing father."

319. "So you're not bothered any more with relatives coming and staying?" asked Jim.

"No," answered Tom with satisfaction. "I borrow money from the rich ones and lend it to the poor ones, and none of them come back."

320. The warden of one of the more advanced prisons began to feel sorry for one of the prisoners. On visitors' day, while most of the prisoners received kinfolk and such, this fellow sat alone in his cell.

One visiting day, the warden called him into the office. "Ben," he said kindly, "I notice you never have any callers. Don't you have any friends—or family?"

"Oh sure," replied Ben happily, "but they're all in here."

Farm—Farmer—Farming

321. A farmer shipped two rabbits east by motor transportation. The crate arrived with two rabbits. That's fast transportation!

322. A man stopped by a booming oil field in southern Kentucky to give a lift to a man on his way to the county seat. They drove through once beautiful farm land now scarred by bulldozers and drilling rigs, cluttered with pumps and storage tanks. Guessing that his passenger was a farmer living in the area, the driver steered the conversation to the tall tales he had heard of quick riches for both speculators and farmers.

The local man acknowledged that many of the stories were founded on fact. "You own a farm here?" the driver asked. "Yeah" was the reply.

"Any oil wells on it?" "Yeah, three good'uns and they say they'll make 300 barrels a day."

"What in the world are you going to do with all the money you'll be getting?" The farmer gazed for a moment across a machine-scarred field and answered, "Why I'm gonna buy me a farm that ain't got no oil on it."

Father—Son

323. *Thoughtful father:* "If my son is getting as much out of college as his college is getting out of me, he will be a success."

324. "My son's letters always send me to the dictionary," bragged the father of a Harvard undergraduate.

"You're lucky," replied his friend. "My son's letters always send me to the bank."

325. A father was berating his son who was reluctant to do his homework. "When Abraham Lincoln was your age," the father lectured, "he walked 10 miles to school every day and then studied by the light of the fire in his log cabin."

"So what?" the boy rejoined. "When John Kennedy was your age, he was President!"

Fishing

326. It's a crime to catch a fish in some lakes and a miracle in lots of others.

327. A thoughtful wife is one who has the pork chops ready when her husband comes home from a fishing trip.

328. A man who will sit on a pier all day waiting to catch a fish will complain if his wife has dinner 10 minutes late.

329. A fisherman was lugging a fish twice his size when he met another fisherman with a half dozen small ones on a string.

"Howdy," said the first fisherman, dropping the huge fish and waiting for a comment.

The fellow fisherman stared and stared. Then he said calmly, "Just caught the one, eh?"

330. "Young man," said the stern moralist to the boy fishing on the creek bank, "your time must not be very valuable. I've been watching you two hours and you haven't had a single bite."

"Well, stranger," the lad replied, "I consider my time too valuable to waste two hours of it watching another guy fishing when he ain't catching anything!"

331. An old-timer sat on the river bank, obviously awaiting a nibble, though the fishing season had not officially opened. The game warden stood behind him quietly for several minutes. "You the game warden?" the old-timer inquired.

"Yup."

Unruffled, the old man began to move the fishing pole from side to side. Finally, he lifted the line out of the water. Pointing to a minnow wriggling on the end of the line, he said, "Just teaching him how to swim."

332. Two ardent fishermen met on their vacation and began swapping stories about the different places they had fished, the kind of tackle used, the best bait, and finally about some of the fish they had caught.

One of them told of a vicious battle he once had with a 300-pound salmon. The other man listened attentively. He frankly admitted he had never caught anything quite that big. However, he told about the time his hook snagged a lantern from the depths of a lake. The lantern carried a tag proving it was lost back in 1912. But the strangest thing of all was the fact that it was a waterproof lantern and the light was still lit.

For a long time the first man said nothing. Then he took one long last draw on his cigarette before rubbing it out in the ash tray.

"I'll tell you what I'll do," he said slowly. "I'll take 200 pounds off my fish, if you'll put out the light in your lantern."

Folly

333. There's no fool like an old fool—you can't beat experience.

Food

334. *Bride:* "The two best things I cook are meat loaf and apple dumplings."
Groom: "Which is this?"

335. A fellow walked into a restaurant, ordered three hamburgers, two steaks, a shrimp salad, fried rice, a side order of dill pickles and ice cream.

The waitress was amazed. "Boy!" she exclaimed. "You sure like food."

"Matter of fact," said the customer, "I hate it. I'm just crazy about bicarbonate of soda."

Forgetfulness

336. *Husband (who's forgotten) to wife:* "How do you expect me to remember your birthday when you never look any older?"

337. *Professor:* "Jones, can you tell me who built the Sphinx?"
Student: "I did know, sir, but I've forgotten."
Professor: "Great guns, what a calamity! The only man living who knows, and he has forgotten!"

Forgiveness

338. In his autobiography Mark Twain concluded a tirade against a publisher, who had once swindled him outrageously, on a note of forgiveness.

"He has been dead a quarter of a century now," Twain wrote. "I feel only compassion for him, and if I could send him a fan I would."

Frustration

339. A most frustrated fellow was the man who bought a new boomerang and had a terrible time throwing the old one away.

340. A man complained to a friend that he had caught his wife going through his pockets lately and it was making him frustrated.

"But why should it make you feel frustrated?" asked the friend.

"Because," replied the man, "she never finds anything."

G

Gambling. See also Bet—Bets—Betting

341. What often keeps a man from making a fast buck is a slow horse.

342. Lady Godiva was the world's greatest gambler because she put everything on a horse.

343. *Sign over a tailor shop in Las Vegas:*
WHILE YOU'RE HERE, WHY DON'T YOU
HAVE YOUR CLOTHES CLEANED TOO.

344. Have you heard the one about the lawyer who drove his $5,000 Cadillac to Las Vegas and came back on a $100,000 Greyhound?

345. At a Las Vegas gambler's funeral, the speaker asserted, "Spike is not dead, he only sleeps."
From among the gambling friends who were attending came a voice, "I got $100 that says he's dead."

346. A beautiful chapel under construction stopped an admiring passer-by. He fell into conversation with the foreman, and many adjectives later, asked: "What denomination is it?"

"Don't know," said the foreman, "we're building it on speculation."

347. Two men were commenting on a friend's bad luck at the horse races.

"Funny," said one, "how lucky Harry is at cards and how unlucky at the track."

"Nothing funny about it," replied the other. "They won't let him shuffle the horses."

348. "Eddie," said a gambler to his friend, "I must tell you about this guy I met yesterday. He's figured out a system whereby a whole family can live without money."

The other gambler looked up eagerly. "Does it work?"

"No," admitted his friend sadly, "but that's the only loophole in his system."

349. A young married couple spending a week at a famous spa had nothing but bad luck, and on the sixth day were down to their last two dollars and a ticket to the local race track.

"Let me go out there alone today," said the young man. "I've got a hunch."

He picked a 40-to-one shot in the first race, and won. Every succeeding race was won by a long shot on which he had a bet. At the end of the afternoon, he had amassed more than 10 thousand dollars.

On his way back to the hotel, he stopped off at one of the gambling casinos to cash in further on his good luck. Within an hour he had run his bankroll up to a neat 40 thousand dollars at roulette. On the point of leaving, he had a new hunch and the entire 40 thousand went on black.

The ball bounced, rolled and settled. The croupier called "Red!"

The young man made his way back to his hotel room, sat down, and lit a cigarette. His wife asked, "How did you make out?"

"I lost two dollars," he nonchalantly replied.

Garden—Gardens—Gardening

350. The best way to enjoy a beautiful, productive garden is to live next door to one, and cultivate your neighbor.

351. The easiest way to tell the difference between young plants and weeds is to pull up everything. If they come up again, they're weeds.

352. "My garden was such a success this year," boasted a gentleman farmer, "that my neighbor's chickens took first prize at the poultry show."

353. An ad in a London newspaper read: "Sprinkle this magic mixture on your flowerbeds and nothing will grow, thus leaving you with plenty of leisure for other things."

354. A man who was new in the suburbs strolled over to observe a neighbor who was digging a hole in his backyard and said, "That's a pretty deep hole. What are you going to put in it?"

"I am replanting some of my garden seeds," was the quick response.

"But you surely don't need such a deep hole to plant a few seeds," the new neighbor said incredulously.

"I surely do," replied the digger. "The seeds are all inside one of your chickens."

355. A wife who was always nagging her husband to mow the lawn hit on a sneaky new way to annoy him. He got home one afternoon and found her out cutting the grass herself with the new power motor. She was, in short, shaming him before the whole neighborhood.

Furious, he took over and finished the job. When he put the mower away, he disconnected the spark plug so as to make sure she wouldn't be able to pull such a stunt a second time.

Several weeks went by and again he came home only to find her out mowing the lawn again.

"There was something wrong with the mower," she told him, "but I called a repair man and he fixed it. And he only charged $5."

Gift—Gifts

356. "How'd your wife like those back scratchers I sent her for Christmas?"

"You mean that's what they were? She's been making me eat salad with them."

357. A woman who lived far beyond her three-score-and-ten years had been in the habit of having a birthday party every year. Her friends and relatives always remembered her with little gifts which were usually in the form of knick-knacks for the house.

Finally arriving at the age of ninety, the old lady was asked by a friend what she wanted for her birthday this year.

"Give me a kiss," was the reply, "so I won't have to dust it."

Giving

358. When it comes to giving, some people stop at nothing.

359. 'Tis much better to give than to receive—and it's deductible.

360. The trouble with some folks who give until it hurts is that they are so sensitive to pain.

361. A recent appeal by a famous neurological institute asked doctors to bequeath their brains for research.

It ended: "any contributions, however small, will be gratefully appreciated."

362. Horace Greeley was once approached for a donation, the purpose of which was to save millions of his fellowmen from going to hell.

"I'll not give a damned cent," Greeley fired back. "Not half enough of them go there now."

Gold-digger—Gold-diggers—Gold-digging

363. One way for a girl to get a mink coat is to find a wolf and skin him.

364. When one beautiful gold-digger asked another why a girl of her age and talents would marry a wealthy old man, she replied:

"Listen, if anyone offered you a check for $1,000,000, would you stop to look at the date?"

Golf

365. By the time a man can afford to lose a golf ball, he can't hit that far.

366. Golf is a lot like taxes—you drive hard to get to the green and then wind up in the hole.

367. One of the quickest ways to meet new people is to pick up the wrong ball on a golf course.

368. Funny, isn't it? Men blame fate for other accidents, but feel personally responsible when they make a hole in one.

369. "I see where a Russian says he has invented a game which closely resembles golf."

"That must be the game my husband has been playing for years."

370. "I'd move heaven and earth to be able to break 100 on this course," sighed Mac, the golfer.

"Try heaven," advised the caddie. "You've already moved most of the earth."

371. A businessman's wife berated him on account of his devotion to the links. "If you keep spending so much time playing golf," she nagged, "you won't have anything set aside for a rainy day."

"I won't, hey?" he replied. "My desk is loaded with work I've got put aside for a rainy day."

372. A woman was bemoaning the fact that her husband had left her for the sixth time.

"Never mind," consoled the neighbor. "He'll be back again."

"Not this time," sobbed the wife. "He's taken his golf clubs this time."

373. A golfer, trying to get out of a trap, said to a fellow player:

"The traps on this course are very annoying, aren't they?"

The second golfer, trying to putt, replied:

"They are, indeed, so would you please close yours?"

374. He had just come in from a long afternoon at golf. His wife kissed him and remarked that their son had just come in, too.

"He says he's been caddying for you," she remarked.

"By golly," exclaimed the golfer, "no wonder that kid looked so familiar!"

375. "Why don't you play golf with George any more?" Pete's wife asked him.

"Would you play with a fellow who puts down the wrong score and moves the ball when you aren't watching?" replied Pete.

"No," she replied, "I certainly wouldn't."

"Neither will George."

376. Sam, innocent of all golfing lore, watched with interest the efforts of the man in the bunker to get himself out.

At last the ball rose in a cloud of sand, hovered in the air and then dropped on the green and rolled into the hole.

"Gosh," said Sam with a chuckle, "he'll have a tough time getting out of that one."

377. The parson was out on the course and thought that it might not be a bad time to slip in a quick moral observation to his partner.

"I have observed," he said, "that the best golfers are not addicted to bad language."

His partner swept a load of topsoil into space and, looking down, said: "What the hell have *they* got to swear about?"

378. Two golfing enthusiasts were discussing their scores in the locker room. "I can't understand it," said one disgustedly, "I've been playing golf for twenty years and I get worse every year. Believe it or not, last year I played worse than the year before. And the year before, I was worse than the last year."

"That's too bad," commented the other. "How are you doing now?"

"I am already," said the man unhappily, "playing next year's game."

379. It was Saturday morning and while they were having breakfast, Mr. Smith suddenly announced that he didn't have to go to the office that morning.

"Well, don't think," said the wife, "that you're going to run off to play golf today and leave me alone with all this work to do."

"Why, golf is the furthest thing from my mind," replied the husband, gnawing at his breakfast, "and please pass me the putter."

380. All summer Paul watched Eddie give demonstrations on how to putt. Ed, who sometimes wears glasses, seldom missed a putt, even from the edge of the green. Finally, at the end of the summer, Paul asked how he holed out so accurately.

"Well," said Ed, "these glasses of mine are bifocals. When I line up a putt, I look through the edges of the two lenses so I see two balls, one small and one big, and two holes, one small and one big. Then it's simple. I just knock the small ball in the big hole."

381. The club's worst golfer was addressing his golf ball. He woggled his driver several times, missed three swings, and finally drove his ball about 20 feet. Looking up in exasperation he saw a squirrel hunter with a gun across his shoulder, who had stopped to watch him. "Look here!" shouted the member angrily. "Only golfers are allowed on this course!"

The stranger nodded, "I know it, mister," he replied. "But I won't say anything if you won't, either!"

382. A group of golfers were putting on the green. Suddenly a ball dropped in their midst. One of the golfers winked at the others, and with his foot shoved the ball into the hole.

A few seconds later a very fat fellow came up to the hole, puffing and out of breath.

"Didja see the ball?" he asked anxiously.

The men said: "Yes."

"Where is it?"

"It went in the hole."

The fat man looked at them unbelieving, walked up to the hole, reached down, picked up the ball. He gazed at it in astonishment, then ran down the fairway and at the top of his lungs shouted, "Hey, Joe. I got a nine."

Government

383. *First farmer:* "Don't think much of that weather prophet the government's got on the radio."

Second farmer: "Well, let's don't do any complainin' about it. Just think how bad it would be if the government started regulatin' the weather instead of predictin' it!"

384. At the check-out counter in a New England supermarket an elderly gentleman unfolded, endorsed and handed to the clerk a rumpled government check on which was plainly printed: "Do not fold, spindle or mutilate."

The clerk looked at it, frowned and said, "You shouldn't do that, Henry. The government doesn't like it."

The old man looked her straight in the eye and replied with emphasis, "Hazel, the government does some things I don't like, too."

Grandparent—Grandparents

385. A grandmother recently met her friend and started to ask, "Did I tell you about the cute thing my granddaughter said . . ."

But she was cut short with, "Before you start I warn you that I demand equal time—and I have sixteen grandchildren!"

386. There was a grandmother who was so tickled to learn that her grandchildren were coming for a week that she put a $5.00 bill in the collection plate at church. When they went home at the end of the week, her joy must have been double because that Sunday she put a $10.00 bill in the plate.

387. A wealthy old farmer was having a family reunion with his large family and as they all sat down to the table for a Sunday dinner, the old man looked around at his six big strapping sons and said:

"I don't see any grandchildren around this table of mine. I want you all to know that I will give $10,000 to the first one of you who presents me with a grandchild. We will now say grace."

When he raised his eyes again, he and his wife were the only ones at the table.

Gratitude

388. If you pick up a starving dog and make him prosperous, he will not bite you. This is the principal difference between a man and a dog.

389. The pretty young thing sat in her stalled auto, awaiting help. Two young men walked up and volunteered their aid.

"I'm out of gas," she purred. "Could you push me to a gas station?"

They readily put their muscles to the rear of the car and rolled it several blocks. After a while, one looked up, exhausted, to see that they had just passed a filling station. "How come you didn't turn in?" he called.

"I never go there," the girl shouted back. "They don't give trading stamps."

Habit—Habits

390. "My wife has the worst habit of staying up until one or two o'clock in the morning, and I can't break her of it."

"What is she doing all that time?"

"Waiting for me to come home."

391. A woman driver made a right turn from a left lane and collided with another car. The other driver angrily asked, "Lady, why didn't you signal?"

Without a moment's hesitation, she replied, "Mister, I always turn here."

Honeymoon

392. An old lady in southern Georgia was busy kneading a huge batch of bread. Noticing that her wood fire needed replenishing, she hastily removed her hands from the dough and rushed to the wood pile where she chopped an armload of wood. As she returned her teenage daughter was standing nearby.

"Momma," she said dreamily. "How long does a honeymoon last?"

" 'Til there's dough on the axe handle, Honey," the old lady replied grimly, " 'Til there's dough on the axe handle."

393. A Scotsman, dressed in his clan tartan, was standing on the platform of Kingsbridge railway station, Dublin, when another kilted Scot came along and inquired, "Where you bound for?"

"I am going to Killarney on my honeymoon," was the reply. "Where is the wife?"

"Am no' taking her," said the bridegroom. "She has been there before, so I left her at home."

Horse racing

394. One man has discovered how to bring home money from the tracks. Instead of picking horses, he picks pockets.

395. "I just crossed a horse with a fish."
"How did you do that?"
"I put a fin on a horse's nose."

396. "Now, don't tell stories, Jimmy. You know your father never took you to the zoo in his whole life."

"Yes, he did, Mommy, and one of the animals paid twenty-seven dollars!"

397. *Blonde:* "My, but the horses in the next race have peculiar names."

Betting man: "Just wait until you hear what the losers call them after the race."

398. Father looked up from his racing form and noticed the baby in the buggy. Turning to his wife he said, "Baby's nose is running again."

His wife snorted and snapped, "Don't you ever think of anything except horse races?"

399. Men are certainly queer. They have always known that one horse can run faster than another, and yet they squander millions of dollars each year to see that simple fact demonstrated over and over again.

400. "Father," asked the small boy, "which can go faster, horses or buses?"

"Buses, of course," replied the father impatiently.

"Then why," asked the boy, "don't you bet on the buses?"

401. A westerner entered an eight-year-old horse in a race at an eastern track. Since the horse had never raced before, he went off at odds of 80 to 1. But he galloped home first by several lengths.

The stewards naturally were suspicious and called in the owner. "How come you never raced this horse before?" they demanded. "After all, you've had him for eight years."

"Well, to tell you the truth," the westerner said sheepishly, "we couldn't catch him until he was seven."

Hospitality

402. The eager-to-please hostess turned to the guest of honor and gushed: "I suppose I can't offer you wine. You are the head of the Temperance League, aren't you?"

"No," he replied, "I'm head of the Anti-Vice League."

"Well," the flustered hostess explained, "I knew there was something I wasn't supposed to offer you."

403. A two-fisted ward boss named Pat Murphy sometimes received invitations to the parties and sometimes was left out. When one of the victory parties to which he had not been invited came off, Pat was almost the first man to appear.

"Why, Pat," said one of his friends, "How come you're here? I understand you were not invited."

"I know it," smiled the Irishman as he reached for a mug

of beer and a sandwich, "but I thought I'd show up just the same, to prove I wasn't mad at not being asked."

Host—Guest

404. The hostess gown was designed to keep you from running down the party to the wrong person.

405. Don't try to make your guests feel at home. If they wanted to feel at home, they would have stayed there.

406. "Does your wife know you're bringing me home for dinner?"

"Does she know it? We argued about it for half an hour this morning."

407. *Visitor:* "Do you like reciting, dear?"
Child: "Oh, no, I hate it, really. But Mommy makes me do it when she wants people to go."

408. George Washington had been visiting in the home of friends and the hour came for him to leave. After saying good-bye to the adults, he paused at the entrance where a little girl opened the door to let him out.

Washington bowed to her and said, "I am sorry, my little dear, to give you so much trouble."

She replied, "I wish, sir, it was to let you in."

409. One blistering, hot day when they had guests for dinner, a mother asked her four-year-old son to say grace before the meal.

"But I don't know what to say," the boy exclaimed.

"Oh, just say what you hear me say," the mother replied.

Obediently, the boy bowed his head and murmured: "Oh, Lord, why did I invite those people here on a hot day like this?"

410. Mrs. Ronnie Greville once gave a cocktail party for about thirty guests, including Sir Austen Chamberlain, then foreign secretary, and his wife.

Mrs. Greville's butler was obviously not quite himself. Reluctant to make a scene, she handed him a note which said: "Leave the room at once. You are drunk."

This analysis was evidently accurate. The butler promptly handed the note, on a salver, to Lady Chamberlain.

Hotel—Hotels

411. *Guest to bellboy:* "Quick! Run up to room 415 and see if I left my pajamas and razor in the bathroom. I'm waiting for a taxi to the airport."

Bellboy (five minutes later and out of breath): "Yes, sir, they're up there!"

412. A tall gaunt-looking man recently entered a small hotel in a town where several fires had occurred, and applied for a room at a price which entitled him to lodging on the top floor. Among his belongings the proprietor spotted a coil of rope, and asked what it was for.

"That's a fire escape," the man said. "I carry one with me so I can let myself down from the window without troubling anyone."

"That's a good plan," said the landlord, "but guests with personal fire escapes like that pay in advance at this hotel."

Hunting

413. Did you hear about the hunter who climbed through the fence with his gun cocked? He is survived by his wife, three children and a rabbit.

414. *Neophyte hunter:* "I shot an elk."
Friend: "How do you know it was an elk?"
Hunter: "By his membership card."

415. An exhausted hunter stumbled into the arms of a fellow hunter: "Am I glad to see you. I've been lost for two days."
"Don't get too excited, friend. I've been lost for two weeks."

416. "Yes," asserted the big game hunter at a cocktail party, "I used to shoot tigers in Africa."
One of his listeners protested, "But there are no tigers on that continent."
"Of course not," glibly replied the hunter, "I shot them all."

Husband—Wife

417. Nothing makes a little knowledge so dangerous as thinking your wife doesn't have it.

418. *Overheard at an auction sale:* "Sold to the lady with her husband's hand over her mouth."

419. When a man displays strength of character in his own home, it's called stubbornness.

420. Many men disappear because they know they're not wanted. And others because they know they are.

421. *Husband (to wife trying on new hat):* "Of course, you can buy it, dear. I like that middle-aged look it gives you."

422. *Wife:* "I've changed my mind."
Husband: "Thank heaven. Does it work any better now?"

423. The average husband can't afford to win an argument from his wife. It costs more to get her to stop crying than what she wanted in the first place.

424. "Few women have any knowledge of parliamentary law."

"You don't know my wife. She's been speaker of the house for twenty-five years."

425. *Wife (gossiping to neighbor as husband washes dishes):* "If you go about it the right way, you can take a lot of drudgery out of housework."

426. A midwest sales manager announced a new sales-incentive contest to his staff. First prize was to be a trip to Hawaii with all expenses paid. Second prize? The same thing, except that it included the salesman's wife.

427. A mild little man returned from his wife's funeral on a windy, stormy day. He had just reached home when a tile was blown from the roof and hit him on the head. "My," he exclaimed, "she certainly got to heaven fast!"

428. A woman in the back seat of a car was haranguing her husband who sat behind the wheel. "And furthermore, Henry," she finished, "when we are driving, it is not necessary to preface every remark you make with 'Pilot to Navigator.'"

429. "How can you talk to me like that," she wailed, "after I've given you the best years of my life?"

"Yeah?" returned the husband. "And who made them the best years of your life?"

430. "Your husband says he leads a dog's life."

"Yes, it's very similar. He comes in with muddy feet, makes himself comfortable by the fire, and waits to be fed."

431. *Maid:* "Your husband, ma'am, is lying unconscious in the hall with a piece of paper in his hand and a large box by his side!"

Mrs. Green (joyfully): "Oh, then my new hat has arrived!"

432. After a very trying day at the office, the husband was enjoying his pipe and reading the evening paper. His wife, who was working on a crossword puzzle, suddenly called out, "John, what is a female sheep?"

"Ewe," replied her husband . . . And that's how the fight began.

433. A woman tourist in Greece rented a car and drove out to one of the ancient temples crumbling under the centuries. Posing near one huge fallen column, she asked a fellow tourist to take a snapshot.

"Don't get the car in the picture," she said, "or my husband will think I knocked this place down."

434. A man appeared in a newspaper office to place an ad offering $100 for the return of his wife's cat.

"That's an awfully high price for a cat," the clerk suggested.

"Not for this one," said the man. "I drowned it."

435. *Wife:* "I've got you this bottle of hair tonic, darling."
Husband: "But my hair isn't falling out."
Wife: "I know, but I want you to give it to your typist at the office; her hair is coming out rather badly."

436. *Housewife:* "Do you mind escorting me out to the garbage can, dear?"
Husband: "Why that?"
Wife: "I want to be able to tell the neighbors that we go out together once in a while."

437. "George," she said to her husband as he arrived home from business that evening, "that diamond ring of mine has somehow worked loose off my finger and I can't find it anywhere."

"It's all right, my dear," he replied. "I came across it in my trousers pocket."

438. Johnny's teacher wrote to his mother: "Johnny is a bright boy, but he seems to spend all his time thinking about girls."

Johnny's mother wrote back to his teacher: "If you find a cure, let me know. I'm having the same trouble with his father."

439. *Wife:* "I mended that hole in your pocket last night after you'd gone to bed, dear. Now, I ask you, am I not the thoughtful little wife?"

Husband: "Well, yes, you're thoughtful enough, but tell me, dear, how did you discover there was a hole in my pocket?"

440. At the big publicity cocktail party, a pretty little blonde waitress went around with a tray of cocktails. Late in the evening, a woman guest asked the host, "Pardon me, but have you seen the girl with the martinis?"

"I'm so sorry," replied the host. "Do you want a drink?"

"No," said the woman. "I want my husband."

441. "How'd you come out in that fight with your wife?"

"She came crawling to me on her hands and knees."

"Yeah? What did she say?"

"Come out from under that bed, you coward!"

442. "You know, dear," he said breaking the long silence. "I've been thinking over our argument."

"Well," she snapped, without looking up from her reading.

"Yes, dear, I've decided to agree with you after all," he said meekly.

"That won't do you any good," she sniffed. "I've changed my mind."

443. A fellow came into a bar and ordered a martini. Before drinking it, he removed the olive and carefully put it into a glass jar. Then he ordered another martini and did the same thing.

After an hour, when he was full of martinis and the jar was full of olives, he staggered out.

"Well," said a customer. "I never saw anything as peculiar as that!"

"What's so peculiar about it?" the bartender said. "His wife sent him out for a jar of olives."

444. *Husband in movie:* "Can you see, dear?"
Wife: "Yes."
Hubby: "Is there a draft on you?"
Wife: "No."
Husband: "Is your seat comfortable?"
Wife: "Yes."
Husband: "Let's change seats."

445. A widow recently married to a widower was accosted by a friend who laughingly remarked: "I suppose, like all men who have been married before, your husband sometimes talks about his first wife?"

"Oh, not any more, he doesn't," the other replied.

"What stopped him?"

"I started talking about my next husband."

I

Identification—Identity

446. How to identify a car owner: He's the one who—after you pull the door shut—always opens it again and slams it harder.

447. Mrs. Trent, seated in her living room, heard the back door slam. Thinking it was her young son, she called: "I'm in here, darling. I've been waiting for you."

There was no answer for a moment. Then a strange voice faltered: "I'm sorry, but I ain't your regular milkman."

448. Artist Pablo Picasso surprised a burglar at work in his new chateau. The intruder got away, but Picasso told the police he could do a rough sketch of what he looked like. On the basis of his drawing, the police arrested a mother superior, the minister of finance, a washing machine, and the Eiffel tower.

449. He took a coed to see her first basketball game and was explaining things to her:

Student: "See that fellow in the middle of the floor? He's the center and that one over there is forward."

Coed: "Yeah, and see that one in the other corner? He's forward, too—I've been out with him."

450. "My, how you've changed. You used to have thick, black hair and now you're bald. You used to have a florid complexion, and now you're pale. You used to be chunky, and now you're skinny. I'm really surprised at your change, Mr. Jones."

"But I'm not Mr. Jones."

"Heavens! You mean to say you've changed your name, too?"

451. Two lawyers were arguing a case in court and began to call each other names.

"You're a loop-brained shyster," roared one.

"And you're an ambulance-chasing cockroach," roared the other.

The judge finally rapped for order. "Now that you two fellows have introduced each other to this court," he said, "you may proceed with the case."

452. John Smith witnessed a minor holdup. In due time police arrived, and one officer asked the witness his name.

"John Smith," said Smith.

"Cut the comedy," snapped the cop. "What's your name?"

"All right," said Smith, "put me down as Winston Churchill."

"That's more like it," said the officer. "You can't pull that John Smith stuff on me!"

453. Harold Hoffman, one-time governor of New Jersey, was an excellent storyteller. He used to swear this one happened:

An old colored state employee was driving a truck along a New Jersey highway and was exceeding the speed limit. A trooper flagged him down and said: "Do you realize you were doing fifty-five miles an hour?"

"No, I didn't," said the old man.

"Haven't you a governor on that truck?"

"No, sir," said the employee, "the governor's in Trenton—that's fertilizer you smell."

454. A legislative committee was assigned to investigate conditions in a mental hospital in an eastern state. There was a dance the evening of the day the committee arrived, and the members were invited to attend.

During the course of the dance, a legislative member took for his partner a pretty patient, to whom he had been introduced by a supervisor. "I don't remember having seen you before," she inquired. "How long have you been a patient here?"

"Oh, I'm not a patient," said the legislator. "I'm a member of a special legislative committee which came down here today to investigate the hospital."

"Of course," returned the lady patient. "How stupid of me. However, I knew the moment I saw you, you were either a member of the legislature or an inmate, and for the life of me I couldn't figure out which."

Ignorance

455. An elderly lady and a young man were the only two passengers to leave the New York subway train at that station. The young man with his quick, long stride reached the exit gate long before the less agile woman. But there he stood, patiently holding the gate open for her. Upon reaching the gate, the lady smiled appreciatively and said, "Thank you so much. I'm really not accustomed to such good manners here in New York."

The young man tipped his hat courteously and replied, "You'll have to excuse me, ma'am. I'm from out of town myself and don't know any better."

456. Learned counsel was addressing a judge who was obviously extremely hostile to the cause being pleaded. Nevertheless, counsel persisted in his argument, which was long and involved and highly technical. The judge heard him out with not very good grace, and when he had concluded could not resist saying, sneeringly: "Mr. Prodder has spoken at great length and with a good deal of eloquence, and I know it must pain him when I say that I, for one, have been left as ignorant as ever." Quick as a flash, counsel was on his feet and retorting: "Ignorant —yes, m'lud, but surely a good deal better informed."

Illusion

457. "Miss Henderson," said the boss, "I want you to prepare a statement for the press announcing that beginning March first this company will pay a pension of $300 a month to all employees who have been with us 20 years or longer."

"But, Mr. Allmant, this company has been in business for less than six months!"

"I know, But it'll look good in the papers anyhow."

458. In his youth the American sculptor Gutzon Borglum studied art in Paris. Like most students he had a hard time making ends meet. When winter came, his studio was bitterly cold, but since he was unable to buy fuel, he had to rely on his imagination to keep him warm.

He would place a lighted candle in the stove and cover the door with a strip of red isinglass. The rosy glow gave such an illusion of warmth that he was able to continue his work without too much discomfort.

Illustration

459. *Judge:* "It is utterly incomprehensible to me how you could kill the man with one blow of your bare fist!"

Accused: "Shall I show you how I did it?"

460. A physician who was asked the difference between rheumatism and gout, answered: "If you take a vise, put a finger between, and turn until you can't stand it any longer, that's rheumatism; if you turn once more, that's gout."

Imitation

461. Little Herbert had bought Grandma a book for her birthday and wanted to write a suitable inscription on the flyleaf. He racked his brain until suddenly he remembered that his father had a book with an inscription of which he was very proud, so Herbie decided to use it.

You can imagine Grandma's surprise when she opened her book, a Bible, and found neatly inscribed the following phrase: "To Grandma, with the compliments of the author."

462. A man had a Chinese plate he valued very much. One day it fell and cracked down the middle. He ordered six more made and to insure the exact pattern, he sent his broken plate as a copy. Wnen he received the package from China six months later, he was astonished to find the Chinese craftsman had so faithfully followed his copy that each new plate had a crack right down the middle.

Moral: If we imitate even the best of men, we are bound to follow some of their imperfections.

Impatience

463. There is the story of the Sunday school teacher who asked a little boy if he knew where God's home was, confidently expecting that he would answer: "In heaven."

"In the bathroom at my house," replied the child.

"Why do you say that?" inquired the shocked teacher.

"Because every morning my daddy pounds on the door and says, 'My lord, are you still there?' "

464. A wealthy manufacturer of 72 married an 18-year-old model. They honeymooned in Miami. After the honeymoon the manufacturer came down with a coronary. He was hospitalized and placed in an oxygen tent. His 18-year-old wife came to visit him.

When he saw her, the manufacturer began to speak. "Darling," he said, "I don't want you to worry about the future. My will has been made. You're going to get all my stocks and bonds, our house in Larchmont, the three cars, the property in Chicago, the villa in Monte Carlo, and a million-dollar trust fund."

Tears welled up in the wife's eyes. "Oh! Fred," she mumbled. "You've been so sweet to me, so kind. Tell me, husband dear, isn't there something I can do for you?"

"Yes," said the husband. "Take your finger away from the opening and let some oxygen into the tent."

Inadequacy

465. Two cows were grazing alongside a highway when a tank-truck of milk on its way to the distributor happened to pass by. On one side of the truck in big red letters was a sign which read, "Pasteurized, homogenized, standardized, Vitamin A added."

One cow turned to the other and remarked, "Makes you feel sort of inadequate, doesn't it?"

Income tax

466. An income tax form is like a laundry list—either way you lose your shirt.

467. The taxpayer no longer fears that Congress will let him down; he just hopes it will let him up.

468. We aren't certain who thought up that $600 tax deduction for a wife, but he must have been a bachelor.

469. America is the only country where it takes more brains to make out the income tax return than it does to make the income.

470. An Internal Revenue man is writing a book called, *"How We Made $1,800,000 off the Fellow Who Wrote a Book About Making $2,000,000 in the Stock Market."*

471. "Look," said the businessman to his accountant. "Let's stop all those tricks. I want to pay my income tax in one lump."

"But you are permitted by law to pay it quarterly," the accountant explained.

"I know that," the boss replied. "But my heart can't take it four times a year."

472. Two income tax collectors died and arrived at the pearly gates. Just ahead of them were two clergymen, but St. Peter motioned them aside and took the internal revenuers into heaven at once.

"Why them ahead of us?" the surprised men of the cloth asked. "Haven't we done everything possible to spread the good word?"

"Yes," said St. Peter, "but those two internal revenue men scared hell out of more people than you ever did."

Inflation

473. A few more years and a dollar-pincher will mean the same thing that a penny-pincher meant a generation ago.

474. Two shoppers in the supermarket were discussing inflation. The first woman remarked, "At least it has one point in its favor."

"Just what can be good about inflation?" asked the other.

"Well, these days it is almost impossible for the kids to get sick on a 5-cent candy bar."

Installment purchase

475. A sign in the gift shop read, "For the man who has everything: a calendar to remind him when the payments are due."

476. "You pay a small deposit," said the salesman, "and then make no more payments for six months."
"Who told you about us?" demanded the lady of the house.

477. Have you heard the one about the rube who walked into the dealer's showroom with a shoebox full of hundred dollar bills and tried to buy a tractor? The salesman could tell him the monthly payments but he didn't know the cash price. The bookkeeper quit because she didn't know how to record the transaction, and the sales manager cancelled the sale because he didn't have a credit report.

Insurance

478. Some weeks after receiving a $1,200 check for the loss of her jewelry, an elderly woman informed her insurance company that she had found the missing property in her cupboard.
"I didn't think it would be fair to keep both the jewels and the money, so I think you will be pleased to know that I sent the $1,200 to the Red Cross."

479. Two vacationing businessmen were comparing notes on the beach at Miami. One said, "I'm here on the insurance money I collected—got $50,000 for fire damage."
"Me, too," the second merchant said. "But I got $100,000 for flood damage."

There was a long thoughtful pause and then the first man said, "Tell me, how do you start a flood?"

480. The man informed the insurance agent that he wished to have his life insured.

"Do you drive a car?" asked the agent.

"No," replied the man.

"Do you often ride in buses or taxis?"

"No."

"Do you fly much?"

"No."

"Well, I'm very sorry, sir," the agent said firmly, "but we don't insure pedestrians."

Integrity

481. *Father (looking over report card) to small boy:* "One thing in your favor—with these grades, you couldn't possibly be cheating."

482. "My grocer gave me a phony quarter this morning. You can't trust anyone these days."

"Let's see it."

"I can't. I passed it at the drug store."

483. Alexander H. H. Stuart and Daniel Webster were both members of President Fillmore's cabinet. One day, on coming home, Stuart found in his hall a brace of ducks with Mr. Webster's name on them.

Knowing they were left by mistake, he told his coachman to take them to Webster's house and tell him the facts. In time the coachman returned with the ducks.

"I have delivered your message to Mr. Webster," said the coachman. "I told him the ducks were left at your house by mistake."

"What did he say?" asked the puzzled Stuart.

"Well, sir," replied the coachman, "Mr. Webster told me to take the ducks back to you and thank you for being more honest than he is, for *your* ducks, which were left at *his* house by mistake, are already on the fire."

Interpretation

484. It was Sunday morning. He slipped into his wife's dressing-gown and went downstairs to answer the door bell. As he opened the door, the milkman kissed him.

After giving due consideration to this unusual occurrence, he came to the conclusion that the milkman's wife must have a similar dressing-gown.

485. A dignitary, visiting Africa, made an appearance before a large gathering of natives. He launched into a long, rambling anecdote that went on for the better part of a half hour. The natives were respectfully silent.

When he had concluded, his interpreter rose and said four words. Everyone laughed uproariously.

The dignitary was stunned. "How could you tell my story so quickly?" he gasped.

"Story too long," said the interpreter. "So I say—'He tell joke. Laugh.'"

Introduction of speaker

486. *Chairman:* "I never saw this man before tonight. If he's good, let's hear him. If he's not, let's get it over with."

487. For fully fifteen minutes an overbearing Washington toastmaster extolled the virtues of Senator Chauncey Depew. It was becoming embarrassing. Just as the toastmaster paused to grasp for a few more phrases to end his introduction, Mrs. Depew leaned over to her husband and in a voice that was louder than she intended it to be, remarked: "Hello, God!"

The toastmaster folded in a wave of laughter.

Invention—Inventions

488. How come, if necessity is the mother of invention, so much unnecessary stuff gets invented?

489. A Southern Senator, voting against a bill to aid education, argued that the whole thing is a waste. "Science makes it impractical," he said. "Why, I once spent two years learnin' how to read; then they invented talkin' pictures and made the whole thing unnecessary."

J

Joint effort

490. A visitor to a mental hospital was astonished to note that watching over a hundred dangerous inmates there were only three guards. He asked: "Don't you feel these people will overpower the guards and escape?" He got the reply, "No, lunatics never unite."

491. Two moving men were struggling with a big crate in a doorway. They pushed and tugged until they were exhausted but it wouldn't move. Finally, the man on the outside said, "We'd better give up, we'll never get this in."

The fellow on the inside said, "What do you mean get it in? I thought you were trying to get it out."

492. The musician was giving a brilliant concert in a famous old church. As he reached the intermission, he departed in back of the organ for a bit of rest. There he found an oldish gentleman smoking his pipe as he rested from the chore of pumping air for the big organ. The fellow smiled and commented: "We're giving them quite a concert, aren't we?"

This seemed out of perspective to the genius, who put the fellow in his place: "What do you mean 'we', old man? I'm giving the concert!"

He went out front. In came the audience, he struck the pose

with hands raised and let them descend for the next number. There was no sound. He dashed behind the organ. There was the man, smoking his pipe. It dawned on the genius and with a smile he admitted: "You were right, we are giving them a concert."

Journalism

493. They claim that when Arthur Brisbane was asked whether columnists are newspapermen, he replied: "Would you call a barnacle a ship?"

494. *Daughter:* "Daddy, why do all the editors refer to themselves as 'we'?"
Daddy: "So the reader who doesn't like what he is printing, will think there are too many for him to lick."

495. "Could you give me some pointers," queried the journalism student, "on how to run a newspaper?"
"You came to the wrong person," answered the editor. "Ask one of my subscribers."

496. The city editor had just been informed that a wire had fallen across Main Street in a storm. He assigned two reporters to the story.
"No one knows whether the wire is live or not," he said. "So one of you is to touch it and the other to write the story."

497. "What," yelled the city editor as the cub reporter came in empty-handed. "You say there was no story in that big society wedding?"
"Not a word," mourned the cub. "The groom failed to show up."

498. *Film star:* "I told the newspapers that what I wanted most was a little cottage with a husband and at least six children."

Friend: "Goodness, what makes you say such silly things?"
Film star: "The publicity department."

499. *Jones:* "In an Australian newspaper office once I saw over the editor's chair the motto, 'Today's paper lights tomorrow's fire.'"

Smith: "That is to induce a proper humility in the staff?"

Jones: "No, it is to encourage them to take a chance with a story."

500. "What do you mean," roared the politician, "by publicly insulting me in your old rag of a paper? I will not stand for it, and I demand an immediate apology."

"Just a moment," answered the editor. "Didn't the news appear exactly as you gave it to us, namely, that you had resigned as city treasurer?"

"It did, but where did you put it?—in the column under the heading *'Public Improvements.'*"

501. The editor looked over the proofs of the book on child care and decided that the author had used the word "underpants" too often.

So the editor jotted down a notation on his calendar pad to "change underpants" in order to remind the author of this change.

The next morning, the editor's private secretary scanned her boss' calendar, scratched her head and mumbled, "What will that guy want me to remind him of next!"

502. The young man had just left journalism school and got a job on the staff of a local paper. He listened intently to the editor's instructions:

"Never write anything as a fact unless you are absolutely sure about it, or you'll get the paper into trouble. Make it a point to use the words, 'alleged', 'reputed', 'claimed', 'rumored', or 'it was said.'"

The youthful reporter kept repeating this instruction to himself as he went out on his first assignment, and this is his first story:

"It is rumored that a party was given yesterday by a number of reputed ladies. Mrs. Smith, it was said, was hostess, and the guests, it is alleged, with the exception of Mrs. Jones, who says she is fresh from London, were all local people. Mrs. Smith claims to be the wife of Joe Smith, rumored to be the president of an alleged bank."

Jurisdiction

503. Asked to officiate at a friend's wedding ceremony, Justice Felix Frankfurter explained that he did not have the authority to perform the ceremony.

"What!" exclaimed his friend. "A Supreme Court Justice doesn't have the authority to marry people! How come?"

"I guess," replied Frankfurter, "it is because marriage is not considered a federal offense."

504. A group of comedians were dining at Lindy's and mourning the untimely passing of one of their favorite waiters, Sam. Thinking it would be a nice gesture to let him know how much they missed him, the boys decided to contact him in the Great Beyond. So they hired a medium to conduct a seance.

Later that week, they got together at a big, round table. "Sam, Sam," the medium intoned. "Can you hear? Can you hear us?"

There was a pause and the medium tried again. "Sam, Sam, why don't you answer?"

Finally, out of the past and into the darkened room, a thin voice was heard by the group: "Sorry, sir, that ain't my table!"

Justice

505. They had been married just two weeks and he was going through a batch of mail that had arrived that morning.

"Honey," he said, "aren't these bills for the clothes you bought before we were married?"

"Yes, darling," she replied. "You're not upset about it, are you?"

"Well," he retorted, "don't you think it's unfair to ask a fish to pay for the bait he was caught with?"

506. Two police magistrates were driving home together at night, when they were stopped by a motorcycle policeman. They were duly charged and, when their cases came up for hearing the next day, they agreed that each should leave the bench in turn to have his case heard by the other.

The first went to trial, pleaded guilty and was promptly fined ten dollars and costs. When they changed places the second magistrate, after pleading guilty, was rather shocked to receive a fine of fifteen dollars and costs.

"That's a bit unfair," he complained. "I only fined you ten dollars."

"I know," was the reply, "but there is too much of this sort of thing going on—this is the second case we've had today."

507. To a recently arrived immigrant the processes of law and order were baffling. He had the misfortune to be arrested for peddling without a license. Now he stood before the bar of justice with three young ladies arrested for soliciting. When the first young lady gave her profession as "actress" the judge sentenced her to thirty days in the workhouse. When the second said she was "a model" she drew a sixty-day sentence. "And what do you do for a living?" the judge fired at the third girl.

"To tell you the truth, your honor," she answered. "I'm a prostitute."

Taken aback by this burst of frankness the judge said, "Honesty has become such a rare commodity in these parts that for telling the truth I'm suspending sentence. You are free to go." Then he turned to the peddler, his face hardened. "And what do *you* do for a living?"

"To tell you the truth, judge," he replied, "I'm a prostitute also."

Kindness

508. The teacher had asked her small pupils to tell about their acts of kindness to dumb animals. After several heart-stirring stories, the teacher asked Tommy if he had anything to add. "Well," he replied rather proudly, "I kicked a boy once for kicking his dog."

509. Two friends were riding a bus when one noticed that the other had his eyes closed. "What's the matter, Mike?" he asked. "Don't you feel well?"

"Oh, I feel fine," replied Mike. "It's just that I can't bear to see women standing."

Kiss—Kisses—Kissing

510. *She:* "I'm telling you for the last time that I won't let you kiss me!"

He: "I knew you'd weaken!"

511. The young artist kissed his model smack on the lips.

"I'll bet you do that to all your models," she said when she had regained her composure.

"No," he replied, "you are the first."

"How many have you had?" she inquired.

"Exactly four," he answered. "A rose, an onion, a banana, and you."

Know-how

512. The history class was studying the Revolutionary battle of Saratoga which was probably lost because General William Howe chose to remain in Philadelphia. The teacher then asked the class to explain this major British defeat.

"Lack of no Howe," answered a voice from the back of the classroom.

513. It is said that Emerson visited a farm one day and was amused to see a boy from a nearby city trying to put a calf into a barn. He shoved and the calf shoved. When he pulled, the calf pulled the other way. A farm girl, standing nearby, smiled, walked over and put her middle finger into the calf's mouth and gently led it into the barn.

514. A little girl returned from her first day in school and proudly exclaimed, "Mother, I was the brightest one in my class!"

"That's fine, Janie," her mother said, "but tell me how it happened."

"Well," Janie replied, "the teacher told each one of us to draw a picture on the blackboard, and then the others were to guess what the picture was. Mine was the only one no one could guess—but I knew exactly what it was all the time!"

Landlord—Tenant

515. Give a man an inch these days and he'll rent it.

516. A group of American tourists were being guided through an ancient castle in Europe.

"This place," the guide told them, "is 600 years old. Not a stone in it has been touched, nothing altered, nothing replaced in all those years."

"Well," said one woman dryly, "they must have the same landlord I have."

Language

517. A college professor was trying to teach one of his students to use correct grammar. The student wasn't too eager to learn.

"What difference does it make if I say bad or badly?" he asked. "They both mean the same thing."

The professor pointed to a shapely girl who had just passed by and said:

"Son, look at that girl and tell me; are you looking at her stern or sternly?"

518. The visiting American and his English friend were

driving through London when the latter mentioned that his wind-screen needed cleaning. "Windshield," the American corrected him.

"Well, over here we call it a windscreen."

"Then you're wrong," argued the American. "After all, we Americans invented the automobile, and we call this a wind-shield."

"That's all very well, old boy," snapped the Englishman, "but who invented the language?"

Lawyer—Lawyers

519. Did you hear about the lawyer's daughter who told her boyfriend, "Stop, and/or I'll slap your face"?

520. One night when the family was around the dinner table, Alan looked at his father very seriously and asked:

"Daddy, when are you going to stop practicing law and really do it?"

521. Once upon a time the fence between heaven and hell broke down. St. Peter appeared at the broken section and called out to the devil: "Hey, Satan, since all the engineers are over in your place, how about getting them to fix this fence?"

"Sorry," replied Satan. "My men are all too busy to go about fixing measly fences."

"Well, then," replied St. Peter, "I'll have to sue you if you don't."

"Oh, yeah," countered the devil, "and where are you going to get a lawyer?"

Lawyer—Client

522. *Lawyer* (*over telephone*): "They can't put you in jail for that."

Client: "Oh, yeah? Where do you think I'm phoning from—the public library?"

523. "You're a cheat!" shouted the lawyer's client. "You're a blackguard! You've kept me hanging for months and got rich on my case alone!"

"That's gratitude!" said the aggrieved lawyer sadly. "And right after I named my new yacht after you!"

524. Russell Sage, the financier, laid a case before his attorney. When he had finished, the lawyer was enthusiastic. "It's an ironclad case," he said confidently. "We can't possibly lose!"

"I guess we won't sue then," said Sage. "That was my opponent's side of the case I gave you."

525. *Judge:* "You wish your trial postponed because your counsel has been taken ill; but since you were caught red-handed and have confessed the theft, I don't see what your counsel could say in your favor."

Prisoner: "That's just what *I* am curious to hear, your Honor!"

526. A man charged with theft showed up in court without an attorney.

"Do you want me to assign you an attorney?" asked the presiding judge.

"No, sir," said the defendant.

"But you are entitled to an attorney and you might as well have the benefit of his services," said the portly jurist.

"If it's all the same with you," said the defendant, "I'd like to throw myself upon the ignorance of the court."

527. A new lawyer had just opened up his office. "Ah! A client already," he thought as he saw the door opening. "I must impress him."

He picked up the telephone. "No, I'm very sorry, but I can't take your case, even for $1,000," he said. "I'm just too busy."

He replaced the receiver and looked at his caller. "And now, what can I do for you?" he asked briskly.

"Nothing, really," was the reply. "I just came to connect your telephone."

528. The plaintiff in a damage suit had enjoyed very little education in his life and was wholly unused to court proceedings. He was considerably disturbed to see that the defendant corporation had two men from its legal staff on the case.

During the recess for lunch, he turned to his own lawyer and said, "I ought to have a second lawyer on my side."

"What's the matter?" demanded his astonished counsel. "I think I am presenting your case very effectively. In fact, I don't see how we can lose."

The plaintiff stroked his chin reflectively. Then he explained, "I notice the corporation has two lawyers. When one of them is up speakin' for their side, the other is sittin' there thinkin'. When you're up speakin' for our side, there ain't nobody thinkin'."

Laziness

529. The late Ben Jones, top trainer of thoroughbreds, was once asked how he happened to choose his career.

"When I was a boy on the farm," he explained, "I was wild about horses and cows. I knew I would spend my life raising one or the other."

"How did you decide which?"

"That was easy," said Jones. "I didn't have to milk horses."

530. The sergeant looked disdainfully at the new recruits. "Men," he shouted, "I have a nice easy job for the laziest rookie here. Will the laziest man step forward?"

Instantly, all the men stepped forward—all but one.

"Why don't you step up to the front with the others?" demanded the sergeant.

"Too much trouble," drawled the rookie.

Legacy—Legacies

531. A Michigan newspaper reported that a generous gentleman had donated a new loud-speaker to his church in fond memory of his wife.

532. The will of the wealthy, but eccentric, man was being read and the relatives all listened expectantly, especially his playboy nephew. Finally the lawyer said, "And to my nephew, Charlie Jones, whom I promised to remember—'Hi, there, Charlie!' "

533. The head of a large mercantile company had died and his secretary had been notified that on reading his will they found she had been named as one of his beneficiaries.

"Oh, no," she said. "I thought all the time he had one, but it wasn't me, honest it wasn't."

534. "This may be gossip, but I heard Jim Johnson married Sarah Doolittle just because her uncle left her a lot of money."

"Well, I've known Jim a long time, and you can tell 'em for me it ain't so. He would have married Sarah no matter who left her the money."

535. When the will was read, all the relatives of the famous industrialist gathered to hear what he had left them. To his wife went most of the large estate, to some cousins went several thousand dollars, and to various others went lesser but substantial gifts.

"And lastly," read the lawyer, "to my nephew, Henry, who was always telling me that health is far more important to a man than wealth, I now leave the entire contents of my third floor closet—my sun lamp."

Life insurance. See Insurance

Longevity

536. No wonder women live longer than men. Look how long they are girls.

537. One way to live longer is to cut out all the things that make you want to live longer.

538. A reporter, interviewing a man who had reached his 99th birthday, said, "I certainly hope I can come back next year and see you reach 100."

"Can't see why not, young feller," the old-timer replied, "you look healthy enough to me."

Long-windedness

539. Some speakers are like some gamblers—they don't have sense enough to quit while they're ahead.

540. "I am a man of few words," shouted a red-necked House member as he started his second hour of a gusty speech.

"That may well be," snickered a nearby colleague, "but you are keeping them mighty busy."

541. An ambassador, on a mission to Sparta from Perinthus, overdid himself by speaking at great length. "What answer shall I give to the Perinthians?" the diplomat asked.

"You may say," replied the King, "that you talked a great deal—while I said nothing."

542. While Adlai Stevenson was campaigning in California, a woman asked him where he got his coat of deep tan.

"You been playing golf?" she accused him.

"No," replied Adlai, "I got this tan making outdoor speeches in Florida."

"Well," the woman told him, "if you got that brown you talked too long."

Loquacity

543. Talk about others and you're a gossip; talk about yourself and you're a bore.

544. Senator Carter Glass once said of a talkative colleague: "When he gets started, his tongue is like a race horse; it runs fastest the less weight it carries."

Luck

545. David, a second-grader, was bumped while getting on the school bus and suffered a two-inch cut on his cheek. At recess he collided with another boy and two of his teeth were knocked loose. At noon while sliding on ice, he fell and broke his wrist. Later at the hospital, his father noticed David was clutching a quarter in his good hand. "I found it on the ground when I fell," David said. "This is the first quarter I ever found. This sure is my lucky day."

546. A grocer, while delivering orders in his station wagon, ran down and seriously injured an old lady. The lady sued and was awarded an amount large enough to drive the man out of business. After difficult times he managed to accumulate enough to try again. But a few months after opening his doors he struck an old gentleman with his delivery truck. The gentleman sued and collected big damages, enough to ruin him.

On a peaceful Sunday the grocer was sitting in his living room when his little boy entered and called out, "Father, Father, Mother's been run over by a great big bus."

The grocer's eyes filled with tears, and in a voice trembling with emotion he cried, "Thank the Lord, the luck's changed at last."

M

Man—Woman

547. Men say women can't be trusted too far; women say men can't be trusted too near!

548. About the only time a woman really succeeds in changing a male is when he's a baby.

549. A pompous gentleman once asked the sharp-tongued actress, Mrs. Patrick Campbell, "Why do you suppose it is that women so utterly lack a sense of humor?"

"God did it on purpose," Mrs. Campbell answered without batting an eyelash, "so that we may love you men instead of laughing at you."

Marriage

550. For every guy who marries for money there's a gal who marries for alimony.

551. Some men marry poor girls to settle down, and others marry rich ones to settle up.

552. Marriage is like a violin. After the beautiful music is over, the strings are still attached.

553. Marriages may be made in heaven, but a lot of the details have to be worked out here on earth.

554. One good reason why a man should get married: He doesn't then have to blame everything on the government.

555. *She:* "Before we got married, you told me you were well off."
He: "I was and I didn't know it."

556. Marriage would work out better if both sides would operate not only on a fifty-fifty basis but on a thrifty-thrifty basis as well.

557. Two old codgers were chatting on a park bench. Said one to the other: "If they'd have had electric blankets and sliced bread when I was a lad, I'd never have got married."

558. A shoe repair sign advertised a leading brand of rubber heel with a lovely gal remarking, "I'm in love with America's Number One Heel." Under this, in a feminine hand, someone added, "Sorry, sister, I married him!"

559. Recently a Canadian newspaper received this anxious epistle from one of its readers: "I read with trepidation that the Church of England is omitting the word 'obey' from the marriage service in their new prayer book. May I ask if this new church law is retroactive?"

560. After the hillbilly wedding one of the local citizens approached the bride's father and said:
"Hey, Zeke, your son-in-law marched up to the altar as though he had lead in his pants!"
Zeke shifted his chaw of tobacco, spat out of the side of his mouth and replied: "He did."

561. A citizen of ancient Rome sought to divorce his wife, and as a result was severely chastened by his friends, who asked: "Was she not chaste? Was she not fair?"

The Roman held out one of his shoes. "Is it not well made?" he said. "Is it not also new?" And when they had agreed that the shoe was both well made and new, the Roman replied: "Yet none of you can tell where it pinches me."

562. Mark Twain once debated the question of polygamy with a Mormon acquaintance. The discussion became heated, and finally the Mormon resorted to the Bible for his affirmative clincher. "Can you tell me of a single passage of Scripture wherein polygamy is forbidden?"

"Certainly," Twain replied. "No man can serve two masters."

563. He confided to his old friend that life was now empty because, "The woman I love has just refused my proposal of marriage."

"Well, don't let that get you down," comforted the friend. "A woman's 'no' often means 'yes'."

"She didn't say 'no'," came the dejected reply. "She said 'phooey'."

564. A young bride-and-groom-to-be had just selected the wedding ring. As the girl admired the plain platinum and diamond band, she suddenly looked concerned. "Tell me," she asked the elderly salesman, "is there anything special I'll have to do to take care of this ring?"

With a fatherly smile, the salesman said: "One of the best ways to protect a wedding ring is to dip it in dishwater three times a day."

565. A European skeptic called on a rabbi to challenge him on a point the doubter considered an inconsistency in the Bible. "It puzzles me," he said. "When God tested Job, He took everything from him but left him his wife. Why?"

"The answer is simple," said the rabbi. "After God finished testing Job, He returned unto him twice what He had taken away. If Job's wife had also been removed, He would have had to give him two wives. And such a penalty not even God dared to inflict on him."

Married life. See also Husband—Wife

566. The story of some marriages should be told in a scrapbook.

567. Some men wonder how they could live without women. The answer is, cheaper.

568. The quickest way for a man to dry his wife's tears is to throw in the sponge.

569. *Husband:* "I've taken you safely over all the rough spots of life, haven't I?"
Wife: "Yes, I don't believe you have missed any of them."

570. "Dad, guess what? I've got my first part in a play," said the budding young actor. "I play the part of a man who has been married for 25 years."
"That's a good start, son," replied the father. "Just keep at it and one of these days you'll get a speaking part."

571. The hostess was pressing her guests to provide entertainment. "Is there any instrument you can play, Mr. Jones?"
"Not away from home," he replied.
"What do you play at home?" she inquired.
"Second fiddle," Jones muttered solemnly.

572. Into a Chicago club walked a member wearing an unaccustomed coat of tan on his cheeks and forehead.

"Hello, there," called one of his fellow club members. "Been sailing or did you get that on the beach?"

"Neither," came the reply. "I took my vacation at home. You see, our kitchen sink faces south."

573. The young woman in the upper Pullman berth attracted the attention of the man in the lower berth. "Will you get me a blanket?" she demurely requested. "I'm cold."

"Are you married?" the man asked.

"No, I'm not married," the girl replied.

"How would you like to pretend you were married?" he inquired.

"Oh! I think that would be fun!"

"Then go get your own blanket!"

574. Sitting silently at the bar, the man sipped his drink, while on his face was an expression of extreme sadness.

"George," asked a friend, "what in the world is the matter?"

"Oh, I'm having troubles with my wife," George explained.

"What happened?"

"Well, she told me she wasn't going to speak to me for thirty days."

"But," his friend objected, "that ought to make you happy."

"It did," George answered, "but today is the last day."

Medical profession

575. A nurse in the maternity ward asked a young medical student why he was so enthusiastic about obstetrics. He said sheepishly, "When I was on medical rotation I suffered from heart attacks, asthma and itch. In surgery I was sure I had ulcers. In the psychiatric wards I thought I was losing my mind. Now, in obstetrics I can relax."

576. A doctor had trouble with his plumbing. The pipes

in his bathroom began to leak. The leak became bigger and bigger.

Even though it was 2 a.m., the doctor decided to phone his plumber. Naturally the plumber got sore being awakened at that hour of the morning. "For Pete's sake, Doc," he wailed. "This is some time to wake up a guy."

"Well," the doctor answered testily, "you've never hesitated to call me in the middle of the night with a medical problem. Now, it just happens I've got a plumbing emergency."

There was a moment's silence. Then the plumber spoke up. "Right you are, Doc," he agreed. "Tell me what's wrong."

The doctor explained about the leak in the bathroom.

"Tell you what to do," the plumber offered. "Take two aspirins every four hours, drop them down the pipe. If the leak hasn't cleared up by morning, phone me at the office."

Medication

577. The trouble with not taking some kind of pills is that your associates will think you're overconfident.

578. "I knew them danged scientists would keep a-foolin' around until they did something they hadn't oughter," stormed the old man of the hills. "Now look what they've gone and did."

"What's that Paw," asked his wife, "you mean the atom bomb?"

"Heck, no," exploded the old man. "They've discovered something besides likker to cure a cold."

Membership, Club. See Club membership

Mind, Presence of

579. One of the most tactful speeches ever thought up suddenly was spoken by the man who blundered into a bathroom where a woman was bathing and calmly turned and left with the words, "I beg your pardon—sir."

580. During Navy maneuvers, the captain was pushing his destroyer to the limit when a sailor came to the bridge with a message from the admiral. "Read it aloud," beamed the captain.

"Of all the blundering idiots. You nearly rammed the flagship," he read.

The captain pursed his lips, then snapped, "Very well, sailor, go below and have it decoded."

581. An Army driver was chauffeur to a major who was a notorious wolf.

One day, the major saw a lovely girl. "Turn the car round," he ordered. The driver promptly stalled the car.

By the time he had re-started it, the girl had vanished.

"Driver," said the major, "you'd be a total loss in an emergency!"

"I thought I did pretty well," the driver said. "That was my girl."

582. The toastmaster was seated between two distinguished United States senators at a big New York dinner. He rose, and in complimentary language, declared: "Ladies and gentlemen, it is my very high privilege to present to you an old friend; a man who is a staunch supporter of the Constitution. He is regarded in Washington as a friend of the veteran, a friend of business and of labor, a brilliant lawmaker. May I present to you at this time, the Honorable . . . the Honorable . . ."

Here the toastmaster became bewildered. Then, turning quickly from one senator to the other, he sputtered, with a broad flush:

"By the way, which one of you fellows wants to speak first?"

583. A film director had been on location for two weeks and in the course of making the picture had fallen head-over-heels in love with the leading lady. Upon his return, rumors of the affair had reached the director's wife.

On the night of his homecoming, they retired. The director dropped off to sleep, and soon was talking in his slumbers: "Darling, you know I love you. You're more to me than anything else on earth."

Suddenly, he awakened, glanced at his wife's hostile face, and sensed the situation. Immediately he turned over, pretended he was still asleep, and remarked: "Cut! Now bring in the horses."

584. A persistent party member once appeared before President Lincoln and demanded appointment to a judgeship as reward for some campaigning he'd done in Illinois. The President, aware of the man's lack of judicial attributes, told him it was impossible. "There simply are no vacancies at the present time," Mr. Lincoln said.

The man left. Early the next morning he was walking along the Potomac when he saw a drowned man pulled from the river and immediately recognized him as a federal judge. Without a moment of hesitation he presented himself to Mr. Lincoln while the President was eating breakfast, told him what he had seen, and demanded an immediate appointment to the vacancy.

Lincoln shook his head. "I'm sorry, sir, but you came too late," said the President. "I have already appointed the lawyer who saw him fall in."

Mistake—Mistakes

585. A group of ministers and a salesmen's organization were holding conventions in the same hotel. The catering department had to work at top speed serving dinners to both. The salesmen were having "Spiked Watermelon" for dessert. But the harassed chef discovered this alcoholic tidbit was being served to the ministers by mistake. "Quick," he commanded a waiter.

"If they haven't eaten the watermelon, bring it back and we'll give it to the salesmen."

The waiter returned in a minute and reported it was too late—the ministers were eating the liquor-spiced dessert.

"Well," demanded the excited chef. "What did they say? How did they like it?"

"I don't know how they liked it," replied the waiter, "but they were dividing up the seeds and putting them in their pockets."

586. Germany's late Cardinal von Faulhaber of Munich once had a conversation with the renowned mathematician, Albert Einstein.

"Cardinal von Faulhaber," Einstein remarked. "I respect religion, but I believe in mathematics. Probably it is the other way around with you."

"You are mistaken," the Cardinal retorted. "To me, both are merely different expressions of the same divine exactness."

"But, Your Eminence, what would you say if mathematical science should some day come to conclusions directly contradictory to religious beliefs?"

"Oh," answered the Cardinal, "I have the highest regard for the competence of mathematicians. I am sure they would never rest until they discovered their mistake."

587. Following the famous compensation bill, Henry Clay found a formidable opposition arrayed against him for re-election. After addressing a crowd, he was stepping down from the platform to mingle with the voters when he was approached by an old friend named Scott—a great huntsman in the district.

"Well, Henry," said Scott, "I've been with you in six troubles, and I'm sorry I must desert you in the seventh. You voted for that miserable compensation bill and now I must turn my back on you."

"Is that your only objection?" asked Clay.

"It is."

"You are an old huntsman," said Clay, "and have killed many a fat bear and buck?"

"Yes," said Scott.

"I believe you have a good rifle?" continued Clay.

"Yes, as good a one as ever cracked."

"Well, then," smiled Clay, "did you ever have a fine buck before you when your gun misfired?"

"Yes, that has happened."

"Well, now, friend Scott, did you take that faithful rifle and break it to pieces on the very next log just because it misfired once, or did you pick the flint and try again?"

"No, Mr. Clay," laughed Scott. "I picked the flint and tried again. And I'll try you again. Give me your hand."

The crowd also got the point, the story spread and Clay was re-elected.

Modern age

588. They're offering a new course in the more modern schools—stair climbing. It's for youngsters raised in ranch houses.

589. The modern college president has three important problems . . . salaries for the professors, football for the alumni and parking space for the students.

590. The modern home is going to be equipped with the latest in domestic kitchen appliances. You press a button and it lights the gas by rubbing two sticks together.

591. "Daddy, will you give me a half dollar?"
"When I was your age, I asked for pennies."
"OK, give me 50 pennies."

592. A Brooklyn gentleman took his wife to the Newark airport and put her on a plane for Buffalo. After fighting his way through the traffic, he arrived back home and wearily ascended the steps to his home to find a telegram in his mailbox. He opened it and read, "Arrived Safely. Love, Lulu."

593. Two men were watching a big excavation job being done by machinery. "If it wasn't for those machines," said one, "a thousand men might be using shovels."

"Yes," replied the other, "and if it wasn't for those shovels 1,000,000 men might be using teaspoons."

594. The junior executive had been complaining to his wife of aches and pains. Neither one could account for his trouble. Arriving home from work one night, he informed her, "I finally discovered why I've been feeling so miserable. We got some ultra-modern office furniture two weeks ago, and I just learned today that I've been sitting in the wastebasket."

595. A business firm wrote to another corporation, saying, "Our electronic brain has computed that the cost of the work you want done will be . . ."

The following reply was received a few days later:

"As this is more than we anticipated, we would like to suggest that your electronic brain make an appointment with our electronic brain to discuss ways and means of reducing the cost of work."

Modern art. See Art, Modern

Mother-in-law

596. Behind every successful man stands a devoted wife —and a surprised mother-in-law.

597. The modern girl usually gets along fine with her mother-in-law because she can't afford another baby sitter.

598. Sometimes you can't tell if a man is trying so hard to be a success to please his wife or to spite his mother-in-law.

599. A newly-married man found his wife in tears when he arrived home from the office.

"You know that cake I made from mother's recipe?" she sobbed. "Well, I put it out to cool and the cat ate half of it."

"Never mind, darling," he comforted. "I know someone who will give us a kitten."

600. A big game hunter went to Africa with his wife and his mother-in-law. They hired a guide who took them on a safari into the wilds of the jungle. One night, about a week after they were out, the husband and his wife awoke and discovered that mama was missing. After searching an hour for her, they were shocked to find her cowering in a clearing with a huge lion standing over her.

"Oh, what are we going to do?" the horrified wife asked.

"Nothing," answered the husband. "The lion got himself into that fix—now let him get out of it."

601. The young wife was in tears when she opened the door for her husband. "I've been insulted," she sobbed. "Your mother insulted me."

"My mother!" he exclaimed. "But she is a hundred miles away."

"I know, but a letter came for you this morning and I opened it."

He looked stern. "I see, but where does the insult come in?"

"In the postscript," she answered. "It said: 'Dear Alice, don't forget to give this letter to George.'"

Music

602. The village band finished a vigorous and not over-harmonious selection. As the perspiring musicians sank to their seats after acknowledging the applause, the trombonist asked, "What's the next number?"

The leader replied, "The Washington Post March."

"Oh, no," gasped the trombonist. "I just got through playing that!"

603. At a large party a Hollywood hostess decided to sing. In an off-pitch voice she rendered *Carry Me Back to Old Virginee*. She really belted the song, and as she sang, she noticed a distinguished, white-haired guest bow his head and weep quietly. When she finished the hostess approached the old man and said, "Pardon me, sir, but are you a Virginian?"

"No, ma'am," said the elderly guest, wiping away a tear. "I'm a musician."

N

Name—Names

604. "Does this package belong to you? The name is obliterated."

"Can't be mine. My name is Smith."

605. The manufacturer of a mobile outhouse for construction sites has hit upon an ideal name for it. He calls it Johnnie on the Spot.

606. *Assistant:* "Chief, there's an applicant who says he used to make his living by sticking his right arm into a lion's mouth."

Boss: "What's his name?"

Assistant: "Lefty."

607. It's the newspaper headline writers who really decide who will be president. To fit into headline space, names have to be reduced to three letters . . . FDR, HST, Ike, JFK . . . a poor guy named Stanford O. Buckley just wouldn't have a chance.

608. At a dinner party, two women had just been introduced to each other.

"Oh, yes," said one of them very sweetly. "We met two years ago at the Johnson's—I'm terribly bad at remembering names, but I never forget a dress."

609. The young wife was pleased to have her husband call her an angel. Unaccustomed to such compliments, she asked him why he called her that.

"Because," he said, "you are always up in the air, you are continually harping on something and you never have a thing to wear."

610. A mother sat knitting one evening as her daughter was reading a book that gave the meaning of names. As the mother knitted she thought of all the young men who called on her daughter.

"Mother," her daughter remarked. "It says that Philip means 'Lover of Horses,' and James means 'Beloved'. I wonder what George means?"

"I hope dear," replied her mother, "in view of the alarming way that you and George have been carrying on, that George means business."

611. A teacher took over a new class: "What's your name?" she asked one little boy.

"Jule," he replied.

"Not Jule," she said. "You shouldn't use contractions. Your name is Julius."

Turning to the next boy, she asked: "What's your name?"

"Billious," he replied.

612. Three women went to a psychiatrist with their young daughters. The psychiatrist examined the first woman and said, "Madam, you have a deep subconscious urge for money and so you named your daughter Penny."

The second lady, a fat woman, went in and the psychiatrist said, "Madam, you have a deep subconscious urge for sweets and so you named your little girl Candy."

The third woman, hearing this, took her little girl by the hand and said, "Come Schenley dear, we're leaving."

Nature

613. Nature is amazing; who would have thought of growing a fly swatter on the rear end of a cow?

Nudism—Nudity

614. Life's greatest mystery—what a nudist does with his keys after locking his car.

615. An engaged couple, nudists, decided to break up. The reason? "We've been seeing too much of each other."

616. "Why the apple for your trademark?" a client asked his tailor.

"Well, if it weren't for the apple, where would the clothing business be today?"

617. The two young nudists were being shown around the colony. One thing puzzled them . . . an old man wore an ankle-length beard.

"Why do you wear that long beard?" they asked him.

"Somebody's got to go out for coffee," was the answer.

618. A midwest farmer got fed up with the cars which constantly sped past his property, endangering the lives of his children and his livestock. He finally solved the problem by erecting a sign that had cars literally creeping past his place. The sign said: "Slow Down for Nudist Camp Crossing."

619. An elderly Florida gent with a mild heart condition was ordered to lose some weight. A friend spotted him sitting on the beach off the Gulf of Mexico, avidly watching cavorting bathing beauties in little more than bikinis.

"Thought you were told to get some exercise?"

"That's right."

"Well, you'll never get it sitting here on the beach."

"That's where you're wrong," smiled the old gentleman. "I walk three miles every day just to watch them."

Occupation—Occupations

620. Two little girls were discussing their fathers. One, boasting, said, "My daddy is a dentist."

"That's nothing," retorted the other. "My daddy is a civil serpent."

621. Two disillusioned college presidents were discussing what they'd do if they had their lives to live over.

"I think I'd like to run an orphanage," said one. "No parents to contend with."

"I'd rather run a penitentiary," said the other. "No alumni pressure groups."

Outer space

622. Your money goes further these days. In fact, a lot of it winds up in outer space.

623. Rumor has it that the latest guided missile is to be named "Civil Service Servant." You can't fire it, it won't work, and it's costing the taxpayer a fortune.

624. The latest in spacemen landing on earth concerns the sensitive little one who descended on New York recently. Walking by a store window, he looked in and saw a piano.

"Okay, you!" he snarled. "Wipe that nasty smile off your face!"

Overweight

625. You can depend on fat men—they will never stoop to anything low.

626. There are two reasons why women don't wear last year's gowns: They don't want to, and they can't.

627. The best way to lose weight is to eat all you want of everything you don't like.

628. The five-year-old was showing a kindergarten classmate the new weight scale in the bathroom.

"What's it for?" the visitor asked.

"I don't know," the five-year-old replied. "All I know is, when you stand on it, it makes you very mad."

629. "For years I've been weighing myself on one of those scales that hands out little cards. When I started I weighed 140 pounds. Now I weigh 180."

"How come you gained so much?"

"My pockets are full of little cards."

630. A comely young matron stepped on the drugstore scales after devouring a giant sundae and was shocked at what she saw. Promptly she slipped off her coat. The results were still unflattering, so she slid off her shoes. But then she discovered she was out of pennies. Without a moment's hesitation, the lad behind the soda fountain stepped forward.

"Don't stop now," he volunteered. "I've got a handful of pennies and they're all yours."

Parent—Child

631. There is only one beautiful child in the world and every mother has it.

632. The easiest way to teach children the value of money is to borrow some from them.

633. *Father:* "Eat your dinner!"
Child: "Motivate me!"

634. *Baby sitter (greeting the returning parents):* "Don't apologize. I wouldn't be in a hurry to come home either!"

635. One reason there are so many juvenile delinquents today is that their dads didn't burn their britches behind them.

636. Parents spend the first three years of a child's life trying to get him to talk . . . and the next sixteen trying to get him to shut up.

637. "I guess I'm wasting my advice on my son."
"No, you're not. Twenty years from now he'll be using the same advice on his son."

638. *Mama:* "I'm so glad to see you sitting so quietly while your father naps."

Junior: "I'm watching his cigarette burn down to his fingers."

639. "Mary," said her mother reprovingly, "every time you disobey, I get another gray hair."

"Gee, Mom," Mary answered, "so it was you who gave grandma all her gray hair."

640. The Scouts were in camp. In an inspection, the director found an umbrella neatly rolled inside the bedroll of a small Scout. As an umbrella was not listed as a necessary item, the director asked the boy to explain.

"Sir," answered the young man with a weary sigh, "did you ever have a mother?"

641. "How quickly can I learn French?" asked the young woman.

"That depends upon you," replied the teacher. "Why are you in such a rush?"

"We've just adopted a French baby only six months old," she answered, "and we want to be able to understand him when he starts to talk."

642. Like every other president, William Howard Taft had to endure his share of abuse. One night at the dinner table his youngest boy made a disrespectful remark to him. There was a sudden hush. Taft became thoughtful.

"Well," said Mrs. Taft, "aren't you going to punish him?"

"If the remark was addressed to me as his father he certainly will be punished," said Taft. "However, if he addressed it to the President of the United States, that is his Constitutional privilege."

Partnership

643. Two brothers in the retail coal business had an intricate problem. One of them had taken an interest in the history and theory of ethics.

"It's a fine thing for you to study ethics," the first brother said, "but if I study ethics too, who's gonna weigh the coal?"

644. A twenty-year business partnership enjoyed by Sam and Pete ended very abruptly when Sam had to take a week off after catching a virus. On the third day of Sam's indisposition, Pete called from the office and said in an excited voice:

"There's $5,000 missing from the safe, Sam. What shall I do?"

"Put it back," Sam ordered coldly.

645. A story of the mid-nineteenth century tells of the man who, upon meeting a friend, told him he was going into business.

"What sort of business?" the friend asked.

"A partnership," the other replied.

"Are you putting in much capital?"

"No. I put in no capital. I put in the experience."

"And he puts in the capital, is that it?"

"Yes. We go into business for three years. He puts in the capital and I put in the experience. At the end of three years I will have the capital; and he will have the experience.

Percentage

646. Two young male students were discussing the newly-discovered fact that the human body is 92 per cent water. Just then a lovely coed walked by and conversation stopped. In a moment one of the boys resumed the subject by remarking, "Man, she sure did a lot with her 8 per cent!"

647. The doctor explained to Higgins that he had a serious ailment for which an operation was absolutely imperative

The patient turned pale and asked, "Isn't it very dangerous?"

"Yes," the doctor replied. "Five out of six who undergo this operation die, but as for you, you have nothing to worry about."

"Why not?" eagerly inquired the patient.

"Well, you see, you're a cinch to recover because my last five patients died," the doctor reassured him.

Perfection

648. A young American singer making his bow at La Scala was flattered when the discerning Italian audience forced him to return and sing an aria for the fourth time. Completely winded, he finally begged off, saying it was physically impossible to sing it a fifth time.

A voice boomed from the gallery: "You'll keep on singing it until you sing it right."

Point of view

649. What is called "congestion" in the subway is called "intimacy" in a night club.

650. *Mom* (*hearing a crash*): "More dishes, Junior?"
Junior: "No, Mom, fewer dishes."

651. On the way to the hospital a nurse was hitting a pretty fast pace. She failed to heed the stoplight on the corner. John Law caught up with her in the next block. Said he: "Doesn't that red light remind you of something?"

Replied the nurse: "Oh, yes, someone wants the bed pan."

652. Three men of different occupations looked at the Grand Canyon.

The archaeologist said: "What a wonder of science!"

The clergyman said: "One of the glories of God!"

The cowboy said: "A heck of a place to lose a cow!"

653. An outraged three-year-old howled his indignation when his mother told him she was locking the porch gate to keep him in. Sometime later, however, when the father locked the gate to the playroom, the youngster made no objection. Papa explained to his son that the gate was being locked to keep his mother from bothering him.

654. "Look here," said the angry hardware dealer to the salesman, "you told me that those mouse traps you sold me were wonderful for mice but my customers are complaining that they haven't caught a single mouse in them!"

"Well," was the salesman's calm reply, "isn't that wonderful for the mice?"

655. An astronomer once remarked to Bishop Fulton J. Sheen:

"To an astronomer man is nothing but an infinitesimal dot in an infinite universe."

"An interesting point of view," remarked the bishop, "but you seem to forget that your infinitesimal dot of a man is still the astronomer."

656. A young man who recently toured England was telling of his indignation over an incident that occurred when he visited the Tower of London. He said an affable Briton approached him with the remark, "American, aren't you? I thought so, from your accent."

"The nerve of the guy, making a crack like that," exclaimed the American, "when he was the one who had the accent!"

657. A monkey was negotiating for a consignment of coconuts with another monkey who had a reputation as a sharp trader. But they were far apart on price, and the prospective buyer was fuming around in the treetops wondering whether or not to increase his offer.

"Now look, Egmont," said his wife, finally. "You go down there and you stick to your original figure. If he haggles, tell him he's wasting his breath. Be firm, Egmont! Don't let him make a man of you."

658. A friend of mine, looking for a flat to stay in during several months' visit to London, thought he'd found the real thing when he spotted an ad in the local paper. It read: "Lavishly furnished flat with excellent view overlooking shrubs and trees, also large variety of flowers and works of stone. Reasonable rent."

He phoned the number indicated, made an appointment, and went along to view the place. It seemed perfect. Then he glanced out of the window at the view. The flat overlooked a cemetery!

659. A salesman delayed longer than usual by one of his customers could not make his regular overnight stop and had to put up in a small country inn. The next morning at breakfast the smiling innkeeper asked, "Did you enjoy the cornet concert in the next room last night?"

The sleepy salesman shook his head angrily. "Enjoy it! I spent half the night pounding on the wall trying to get that idiot to stop his racket and go to bed."

"There certainly has been a misunderstanding," snapped the innkeeper, his smile gone. "My son told me he hated to disappoint you the way you kept pounding for more, but after he played every piece he knew five or six times, he simply had to stop and get some sleep."

660. An old story tells of two men who were walking along the streets of London, when the music of some wonderful chimes in a nearby cathedral floated through the air. One of the men remarked to the other, "Isn't that wonderful music?"

"I didn't hear what you said," replied the other.

"Aren't those chimes beautiful?" repeated the first speaker. But again the other man failed to catch the words, and the first speaker said for the third time, "Isn't that lovely music?"

"It's no use," came the answer. "Those pesky bells are making so much noise I can't hear what you say."

661. "Look at that one—the one staring at us through the bars. Doesn't he look intelligent?"

"Yes. There's something uncanny about it."

"He looks as if he understood every word we're saying."

"Walks on his hind legs, too, and swings his arms."

"There! He's got a peanut. Let's see what he does with it."

"Well, what do you know about that! He knows enough to take off the shell before he eats it, like we do."

"That's a female alongside of him. Listen to her chatter at him. He doesn't seem to be paying much attention to her though."

"She must be his mate."

"They look kind of sad, don't they?"

"Yes, I guess they wish they were in here with us monkeys."

Police

662. The police station had been quiet most of the week. Things were so slow the detectives were playing cards to pass the time. "What a life," grumbled one of the officers. "No fights, no thefts, no riots, no murders, no nothin'."

"Rest easy, Mike," said the captain. "Things'll break soon. You just gotta have faith in human nature."

663. *Sergeant:* "Did you give the prisoner the third degree?"

Officer: "Yes, we browbeat him, badgered him, and asked him every question we could think of."

"So?"

"He dozed off and merely said, 'Yes, dear, you are perfectly right.'"

Politeness

664. Short skirts have a tendency to make men polite. Have you ever seen a man get on a bus ahead of one?

665. When a man opens the door of his car for his wife, you can be sure that either the car or the wife is new.

666. The pompous and arrogant lady customer in the antique shop was obviously just passing the time, making the owner drag out fragile old pieces and then commenting on their poor quality and high prices. After about an hour of this, she looked at her watch and said she must go.

"I suppose," she said, "that you think I'm a nuisance, just trying to pretend that I know what I'm talking about."

The owner bowed graciously. "If you say so, my dear lady," he said. "In my shop, the customer is always right."

Politics

667. Overheard in a restaurant—one girl to another: "What I'm looking for is a man who will treat me as if I was a voter and he was a candidate."

668. Two political candidates were having a hot debate. Finally, one of them jumped up and yelled at the other: "What about the powerful interest that controls you?"

And the other guy screamed back: "You leave my wife out of this."

669. When the youthful Tom Dewey announced his candidacy for the presidency at the 1940 Republican convention, crusty old Harold Ickes, New Deal Secretary of the Interior, commented: "I see that Dewey has thrown his diaper into the ring."

670. At a victory celebration for his opponent the Congressman who had been swept out of office by a political landslide, was called upon for a few remarks. He rose and dryly said: "I am reminded of an epitaph on an old tombstone in the town cemetery which read: 'I expected this, but not so soon.'"

671. A politician who had changed his views rather radically was congratulated by a colleague. "I'm glad you've seen the light," he said.

"I didn't see the light," came the terse reply. "I felt the heat."

672. We expect to find a doctor practicing medicine, a lawyer practicing law, an engineer engaged in engineering projects, school teachers teaching school; but when it comes to politics, we think there is something reprehensible in the fact that those engaged in politics are politicians.

673. Congressman John Allen once was pleading his case before some hostile voters, a heavy stone was thrown at him, which, as he happened to stoop at that instant, passed over his head.

"You see," he said to friends who congratulated him on his narrow escape, "if I had been an upright politician, I would have been killed."

674. "Well," the little old lady finally admitted to the persistent politician, "you're my second choice."

"I'm honored, ma'am," he gushed. "But may I ask—who's your first?"

"Oh," she said casually, "anybody else who's running."

675. It is alleged that Senator Claude Pepper was clobbered in Florida in 1950 by a reported speech of Senator Smathers, in the illiterate back-country, in which he said: "Are you good folks aware that Senator Pepper is known all over Washington as a shameless extrovert? Not only that, but this man practices nepotism with his sister-in-law and he has a sister who was once a thespian in New York City. Worst of all, before his marriage, Claude Pepper habitually practiced celibacy."

676. Like all political fights, the Jackson-Van Buren contest had its bitter moments. One young voter, at a political rally, cried out: "Three cheers for Jackson!" A Van Buren adherent promptly shouted angrily: "Three cheers for a jackass!"

"Okay," laughed the youth, "we won't quarrel. You cheer for your man and I'll cheer for mine."

677. A Vermonter had seventeen children, all boys. When they came of age, they voted uniformly for the Republican ticket —all except one boy. The father was asked to explain this terrible fall from grace.

"Well," he said, "I've always tried to bring them boys up right, in the fear of the Lord and Republicans to the bone, but John, the ornery cuss, got to readin'."

678. During a California senatorial contest many years ago, one of the candidates was being maligned badly. A voter wired him thus: "A report receiving wide circulation here that your children have not been baptized. Telegraph denial immediately."

The reply came back: "Sorry to say, report is correct. I have no children."

679. A woman was arrested for speeding. The traffic officer asked to see her driver's license. It was a restricted license and it read she must always wear her glasses while driving. The officer seeing she was wearing none, said: "Where are your glasses?"

"But officer, I have Contacts," she replied.

"I don't care who your friends are. I am going to give you a ticket anyway," he said.

680. While campaigning in a rural section of the Midwest for a congressional seat, a politician ran into an unfriendly crowd at one stop, and halfway through his speech was suddenly pelted with tomatoes and over-ripe fruit.

His presence of mind, however, did not fail him, and his next remark as he wiped the missiles off his face and shirt front turned boos into cheers. "My critics," he said jauntily, "may not think I know much about farm problems—but they'll have to admit I'm being a big help with the farm surplus!"

681. Franklin Delano Roosevelt met an old neighbor during the third term campaign. "Whom are you voting for this year?" Roosevelt asked.

"The Republicans," the man said.

"How come?" Roosevelt asked. "Third term issue bothering you?"

"It's not that at all, Franklin," the neighbor said. "It's just that—well—I voted Republican the first time you ran, I voted Republican the second time you ran, and I'm going to vote Republican again because I never had it so good."

682. A Texas oilman offered to throw the biggest gol-darned victory party for Thomas E. Dewey this country or any other country ever saw. "It'll be a two-hundred-and-fifty-thousand-dollar complimentary banquet in honor of Dewey's election to the office of President of the United States," he said.

"Fine," said a friend. "But supposin' he don't win the election."

The Texan replied. "Then we'll have the complimentary banquet in honor of his defeat."

683. Governor Robert Bradford of Massachusetts set down these attributes for a successful politician: "To live long in politics, you must possess the hide of a rhinoceros, the memory of an elephant, the persistence of a beaver, the native friendliness of a mongrel pup. You need the heart of a lion and the stomach of an ostrich. And it helps to have the humor and ubiquity of the crow. But all of these combined are not enough, unless when it comes to matters of principle, you also have the stubbornness of an army mule."

684. George E. Allen, once President Eisenhower's golf

and bridge buddy, said that President Roosevelt liked best this joke on himself. A dyed-in-the-wool New Deal-hater in Westchester commuted to New York daily and damned Roosevelt every inch of the way. Reaching Grand Central, he always rushed to the newsstand, bought a *Times,* glanced over the front page and handed it back to the newsdealer. Finally, the dealer asked him why he never looked at the inside of the paper.

"I'm only interested in finding a certain obituary," the enemy said.

"But the obituaries are on page 24," the dealer suggested.

"The so and so I'm looking for," said the man of firm habit, "will be on page one."

685. The margin of a single vote has been responsible for many of the great decisions, victories, defeats and disappointments of history.

Thomas Jefferson was elected President by one vote in the electoral college. So was John Quincy Adams. Rutherford B. Hayes was elected President by one vote. His election was contested; referred to an electoral commission, the matter was again decided by a single vote. The man who had cast the deciding vote for President Hayes was himself elected to Congress by a margin of one vote. That one vote was cast by a voter who, though desperately ill, insisted on being taken to the polls.

Marcus Morton was elected governor of Massachusetts by one vote. Countless mayors, legislators, councilmen, and other public officials have enjoyed the sweet wine of victory or the bitter gall of defeat by a single vote. California, Washington, Idaho, Texas and Oregon gained statehood by one vote.

The ill-considered War of 1812 was brought about by a series of events based upon a single vote.

Preaching

686. The average man's idea of a good sermon is one that goes over his head—and hits one of his neighbors.

687. The sermon went on and on. Finally, the priest paused and asked, "What more, my friends, can I say?"

From the rear of the nave came a hollow voice: "Amen."

688. During Sunday services the minister told his congregation:

"Today I've prepared a fifty dollar sermon, a twenty dollar sermon and a ten dollar sermon."

After a brief pause, he continued: "We will now take up the collection and see which one it will be."

Precaution

689. There's a manufacturer who lost a fortune in the stock market and now won't even read a book with margins in it.

690. "My good man," said the dentist. "You don't have to pay me now."

"Pay you?" said the patient. "I'm counting my money before you gimme the gas."

691. Forest Evashevski's housekeeper at Iowa was devoutly religious. After a Rose Bowl victory, Hawkeye fans presented Ev with a new car. He drove it home, pulled up in front of his house, and strolled to the front porch.

"What do you think?" Ev asked the housekeeper.

The good woman appraised him silently, then said, "Just remember the same people who praised Jesus also crucified Him."

Premium—Premiums

692. A bride was showing a friend the kitchen of her new, seven-room house.

"We furnished the kitchen with soap coupons," the bride said.

"With soap coupons!" the friend exclaimed. "What about the other six rooms?"

"Oh, those," the bride replied, "they're filled with soap."

Preoccupation

693. *Doctor:* "You've simply got to have more diversion and relaxation."

Patient: "But, doctor, I'm too busy."

Doctor: "Nonsense! The ants are hard-working creatures, but they always take time to attend all the picnics."

694. An Omaha woman, caught short on groceries for her husband's breakfast and lunch, rushed to the store for food. With her she took five-year-old Terry.

"Hey, mom, can I tell you something?" puffed Terry as they rushed to the store.

"No, Terry, I'm too busy," said his mother.

At the store, Terry tried again, "Hey, mom . . ."

"Don't bother me. I'm trying to think," his mother interrupted.

Finally at home, Terry said, "Now can I tell you?"

"Oh, yes, what is it?" said his mother in exasperation.

"I wanted to tell you that the zipper on your shorts is unzipped."

Prevention

695. An English journalist asked the sergeant of police in a Fermanagh village about the size of his staff.

"I have three," said the sergeant.

"With yourself, that's four. Surely there isn't enough work in this small place to keep four of you going?" the reporter asked.

"Well," said the sergeant, "there is not, but if we weren't here there would be."

Profanity

696. *Mother:* "What did your father say when he fell off the ladder?"
Junior: "Shall I leave out the naughty words?"
Mother: "Of course, dear."
Junior: "Nothing."

697. "Boss," said the dock foreman, "the men on the dock are a little leary of the new freight loader you hired yesterday."
"Why so?" asked the terminal manager. "He checked out well."
"Maybe so," replied the dock foreman, "but this morning he stubbed his toe on a crate of iron castings and said, 'Oh, the perversity of inanimate objects.' "

Professional fees

698. A patient once complained to his psychiatrist that he was always forgetting things. "What shall I do?" he asked.
"Pay me in advance," the doctor advised.

699. *Lawyer:* "When I was a boy, my highest ambition was to be a pirate."
Client: "Congratulations!"

700. Upon receiving the bill for the extraction of a tooth, Pete phoned his dentist and complained. "Why that's three times what you usually charge!"
"Yes, I know," replied the dentist, "but you yelled so loud you scared away two other patients!"

701. A physician presented his bill to the courts as a legal way of collecting fees due from a deceased person's estate. "Do you wish my bill sworn to?" the doctor asked.

"No," said the legalite. "Death of the deceased is sufficient evidence that you attended him professionally."

702. "Whenever I have a headache," explained the patient to his doctor, "I take aspirin. When I have a cold, I go to bed and drink fruit juices. If I have stomach trouble, I take bicarbonate of soda. Have I been doing the right things?"

"Yes, you have," replied the doctor. "That will be ten dollars, please."

703. Nobody has made much fuss about it, but the doctors in Beverly Hills, California, are pretty expensive these days. Recently a man fell down a flight of stairs and hurt his leg. He went to the doctor who fixed him up. As he was leaving, the doctor said to him, "Don't worry! You'll be walking before the day is over." He was right. He took the man's car for his fee.

704. There was a pretty young nursing student who broke her engagement to a doctor, and she was telling her girl friend about it.

"Do you mean to say," exclaimed her friend, wide-eyed, "he actually asked you to give back all his presents?"

"Not only that," sniffed the young student, "he sent me a bill for 36 visits!"

705. The prisoner had sent for the town's leading lawyer.
"Have you anything by way of cash for my fee?" the attorney wanted to know.

"No, but I've got a new Ford car."

"Well, that's fine. That will do. And what is the charge they are holding against you?"

The prisoner replied, "Stealing a new Ford car."

706. After giving the new patient a thorough diagnostic

examination and prescribing medicines and special foods, the Park Avenue doctor announced that his fee would be $50.

The visitor blanched, "That's almost as much as I make in a week."

The doctor offered to reduce the bill to $40. Still the man protested. After much haggling, the MD reluctantly accepted $10. "But why," he asked, "did you come to a specialist like me? Why not a charity clinic? That wouldn't cost you anything."

"Oh, no. When I'm sick, money's no object."

Promise—Promises

707. Three turtles decided they would go on a picnic down on the banks of the Willamette River. They packed their lunches and arrived at the river. Before they could begin eating, it started to rain. They decided one must go back after an umbrella so that they could eat in the dry. The smallest turtle was the one who finally agreed to go if the others would promise not to eat the sandwiches while he was gone. It was agreed.

They waited a day, a week, a month, until finally a year had gone by. Still the turtle did not return. . . . Finally, one turtle said to the other, "He's not coming back, let's go ahead and eat the sandwiches." Just then the little turtle stuck his head from behind the nearby rock and said, "If you do, I won't go."

Proof

708. The trouble with being best man at a wedding is that you get no chance to prove it.

709. In a courtroom it takes twelve men to find out if a woman is innocent. On a country lane in the moonlight, it takes only one.

710. "And you still insist you're innocent," repeated the judge, "in spite of the proof that seven witnesses saw you steal the necklace?"

"If it's witnesses you want, sir," replied the defendant, "I can produce seventy who didn't see me steal it."

711. Two men who loved to argue stood on a street curb in Warsaw watching a regiment of infantry march past. For no apparent reason one of them turned to the other and said, "You claim to be a scholar. Can you tell me, do men grow upward or downward?"

"Downward, of course," replied the other.

"How do you know that?" asked the first.

"Very simple," replied the second man. "When I outgrow my overcoat it becomes too short for me at the bottom."

"Ah, but look at those soldiers marching by," said the first one. "Do they not prove that men grow upward?"

"In what way, pray?" asked the second one.

"Because, as you can readily see, they are all even at the bottom and uneven at the top."

Psychiatrist—Psychiatrists

712. "I'm through going to psychiatrists," asserted the cute little blonde. "I just can't get used to a guy who tells me to lie down on a couch and then sends me the bill."

713. A young psychiatrist, haggard with the troubles of his patients, got into the elevator of a New York hospital with an elderly but sprightly senior consultant.

"How on earth do you remain so youthful, sir?" sighed the younger man, "listening year after year to all those terrible complaints, anxieties and fears?"

The older man shrugged his shoulders: "Who listens?"

Psychiatry

714. *Psychiatrist to patient:* "Despite what you think, Mr. Jones, you don't have a complex. Actually, you *are* inferior."

715. *Psychiatrist to male patient:* "Did this feeling of being an insignificant pipsqueak come on suddenly, or did it develop normally with marriage and parenthood?"

716. A psychiatrist recently reported that half his patients went to him because they weren't married, while the other half went to him because they were.

717. A patient was informed by his psychiatrist that he could consider himself cured of his delusion that he was Napoleon.

"Oh, wonderful!" cried the happy man. "Where's the phone? I must call Josephine and tell her the great news."

718. "I see you were last employed by a psychiatrist," said the employer to the applicant. "Why did you leave?"

"Well," she replied, "I just couldn't win. If I was late to work, I was hostile. If I was early, I had an anxiety complex. If I was on time, I was compulsive."

719. A haggard man walked into a psychiatrist's office, tore open a cigarette and stuffed the tobacco up his nose.

"I see you really need me," the startled doctor remarked as he ran toward the man.

"Sure do," said the guy, "have you got a light?"

720. *Psychiatrist to patient:* "That'll be $75."
Patient: "Why $75?" All the others only charge $50."
Psychiatrist: "It's part of the treatment. It will help you to attach less importance to money and material things."

721. A French comedian, Raymond Devos, visited a mental hospital in the French provinces and saw a sad young male patient nursing a doll. "He was turned down by the girl he loved," explained the psychiatrist who was acting as guide-escort.

Just then another, more violent, patient rushed up with several of the staff in hot pursuit. The psychiatrist said, "That's the man who married the girl."

722. A man insisted to his psychiatrist that he had swallowed a horse. None of the doctor's persuasive tactics could persuade him to change his mind. In desperation, the psychiatrist agreed to "operate." The idea was simply to put the patient under and bring a horse into the operating room.

When the patient came to, the doctor pointed to the horse and said: "Well, that won't worry you any more."

"That's not the one I swallowed," he said. "That's a bay. My horse was white.

723. After the psychiatrist had examined the child, he turned to the child's mother and said:

"I will see Johnny in a month again. But you, madam, also need help. You are far too upset and worried about your child. I suggest that you take these tranquilizers regularly until I see you again."

A month later, the mother brought her child to the psychiatrist.

"How is Johnny?" asked the doctor.

To which the mother replied: "Who cares?"

Public speaking

724. If a thing goes without saying, let it.

725. The man who rises to the occasion should know when to sit down.

PUBLIC SPEAKING ★ *166*

726. *Speaker:* "I have only ten minutes and hardly know where to begin."

A voice: "Begin at the ninth."

727. A physician reports the sense of hearing is considerably dulled by eating. Which is nature's way of protecting us against after-dinner speakers.

728. Once upon a time a lion ate a bull and he felt so good that he roared and roared. A hunter heard him and killed him with one shot.

Moral: When you are full of bull, keep your mouth shut.

729. When Thomas Buckley first ran for auditor of Massachusetts in 1941, his speech consisted of but seven words: "I am an auditor," he said, "not an orator." He continued to run and win for years thereafter—with the same seven words!

730. A senator, who shall remain nameless, was approached in the corridor by a colleague, who asked: "How was your speech at the Democratic dinner last night?"

"Well," replied the first senator, with a puzzled look, "when I sat down, the toastmaster said it was the best thing I ever did. Now I'm wondering what he meant."

731. The candidate's wife dropped heavily into an easy chair, kicked off her shoes and sighed: "Boy, what a day—I've never been so tired in my life."

"Why should you be tired?" growled her husband. "Think of me making seven speeches to the voters. You didn't have to do that."

"That's right," agreed the weary wife, "but, remember, I had to listen to 'em."

732. Joseph H. Choate, one-time ambassador to Great Britain, was called upon at a dinner of the Pilgrim Fathers to respond to the toast, "The Pilgrim Fathers."

After paying tribute to the Pilgrim Fathers for enduring the rigors of the New England winters and the privations and dangers of life in the little settlement of ,Plymouth, he paused.

"But let us give thought," he added with a grin, "to the Pilgrim Mothers. For they not only had to endure everything the Pilgrim Fathers endured, but mark this, they had to endure, also, the Pilgrim Fathers."

733. Once when J. Sterling Morton was making a speech, a man in the crowd shouted, "Louder!" Mr. Morton raised a voice which was always more sonorous than a whisper, but the man yelled "Louder!" again.

Mr. Morton once more put on steam, and his voice stretched out to the edges of the crowd as he lambasted the free silver apostasy of his well known political enemy, William Jennings Bryan.

When the man for the third time yelled "Louder!" Mr. Morton paused for a moment and then continued:

"My friends, the time will finally come when the vast machinery of this universe must stop, and all the wheels, gears and belts be motionless, when the spheres shall cease to roll, and the defined periods of time be lost in eternity.

"In that awful hour, my friends, the angel Gabriel will descend from the battlements of heaven, and place one foot on the land and the other on the sea. He will force a blast from his trumpet which will reverberate throughout the remotest corners of the universe. And when he does, some small-bore idiot will holler 'Louder! Louder!'"

Punctuality

734. It's easy to tell those who have never had much experience in committee work—they always get to the meeting on time.

735. "Norah," said the minister to his housekeeper. "I've asked Mr. and Mrs. James to dinner at 6:30, but I think I'll give them a quarter of an hour's grace."

"Well, sir," replied the housekeeper, "I'm religious myself, but I think you're overdoing it."

736. In most Federal offices, contrary to general belief, they set a great store by punctuality. Former Senator Clinton Anderson (D-N.M.) told of an employee who showed up an hour late at the General Accounting Office. The worker limped, was bruised and battered about the face and carried his arm in a sling. His section chief glowered at him and glanced meaningly at the clock.

"I fell out of the window," the timid worker explained.

"And that took you an hour?" his boss roared.

Punishment

737. One of those amateur sopranos who seems to feel the urge to screech away at every opportunity was rendering some numbers in prison before a convict group.

The warden's young son was visiting him that evening and the boy took all this in with some awe. The warden winced a little as she reached for some high notes and he turned to his son and said: "Let this be a lesson to you should you ever feel tempted to do something wrong."

738. Five-year-old Billy ran into the house to tell his mother that four-year-old Johnny had fallen into the fish pond. She ran out to the pond and found Johnny submerged up to his neck and yelling for help. After rescuing him, she asked Billy how it had happened.

"I kept telling him that he was going to fall into the pond if he got too close to the edge."

"But what made him fall in?" demanded his mother.

"I pushed him," was the matter-of-fact reply.

"What?" cried the mother.

"Yes, I pushed him," Billy repeated. "I wanted to show him what would happen if he didn't mind."

Purpose

739. The neighborhood kids had congregated in the front yard when a fire truck zoomed past. Sitting on the front seat was a Boxer dog. The children fell to discussing the dog's duties in connection with the fire truck.

"They use him to keep the crowds back when they go to a fire," said a five-year-old girl.

"No," said another, "they carry him for good luck."

The third, a boy about six, brought the argument to an abrupt end. "They use the dog," he said firmly, "to find the fire plug."

Qualification—Qualifications

740. There's at least one ineligible football star at every college. Same old story—he could run and kick, but he couldn't pass.

741. As the X-ray specialist walked down the aisle to say the marriage vows with a former patient, someone whispered: "I wonder what he saw in her?"

742. Lincoln called in Ben Wade and Senator Daniel Voorhees to discuss the appointment of an Indian commissioner, explaining what kind of man he wanted to appoint.

"Gentlemen, for an Indian commissioner," said the President, "I want a pure-minded, moral, Christian man—frugal and self-sacrificing."

"I think," interrupted Voorhees, "that you won't find him."

"Why not?"

"Because, Mr. President, he was crucified about eighteen hundred years ago," said the senator.

Question—Answer

743. *Small boy:* "Daddy, why does it rain?"
Daddy: "It rains to make the lawn and flowers grow."
Small boy: "Then why does it rain on sidewalks?"

744. The head of a branch of the American Society for the Prevention of Cruelty to Animals had just hired a new typist, and he spent an hour explaining the work of the organization and the office routine.

"If you have any questions as you go along, don't be afraid to ask," he told her before returning to his desk.

A few minutes later the girl appeared in front of him. "I have a question," she said. "Is it all right if I swat a fly?"

745. A pastor of the parish always asked the children the same questions, and in the same sequence: "What is your name? How old are you? Did you say your prayers? What will happen to you if you don't say your prayers?"

An overly ambitious mother rehearsed her little boy with the answers, and when the pastor called, the boy beat him to the punch by rattling off: "Jerry Jones—5—yes—go to hell."

746. The lion was stalking through the jungle looking for trouble. He grabbed a passing tiger and asked, "Who is the king of the jungle?"

"You are, O mighty lion," answered the tiger.

The lion then grabbed a bear and asked, "Who is boss of the jungle?"

"You, O mighty lion," answered the bear.

Next the lion met an elephant and asked, "Who is boss of the jungle?" The elephant grabbed him with his trunk, whirled him around and threw him up against a tree, leaving him bleeding and broken. The lion got up feebly and said, "Just because you don't know the answer is no reason for you to get so rough."

747. A grandfather was alone at home for a few days while his wife visited one of their daughters. To his consternation another daughter came over and left one of his young grandsons to spend the night with him. The next morning grandpop got up and prepared a big bowl of oatmeal, his own favorite breakfast.

QUESTION—ANSWER ★ *172*

"Do you like sugar?" he asked the small boy.

The grandson nodded.

"How about some butter, too?"

Again the boy nodded.

"Of course, you like milk?"

"Sure," the boy replied.

When grandpop placed the steaming bowl of oatmeal with butter, sugar, and milk before him, the boy refused to eat it.

The grandfather was exasperated. "But when I asked you, didn't you say you liked sugar, butter and milk?"

"Yes," replied the youngster, "but you didn't ask me if I liked oatmeal."

748. An old-timer strutted into a saloon and, in a heavy drawl, ordered a mint-julep. The bartender hesitated, but only for a moment before going to work on a concoction which he topped off with a green leaf. Smiling proudly he set the drink in front of his distinguished customer.

The man frowned as he sniffed the drink. He tilted the glass to sample its content, and then slammed the glass down. He stared angrily at the man behind the bar. "Sir," he said, in a much too affected drawl, "is this really a mint julep?"

The bartender looked pained, but only for a moment. "Are you really a Southern gentleman?" he asked politely.

"Indeed I am, sir," the man hastened to reply.

"Then," snapped the barkeep, "you shouldn't have had to ask."

Real estate

749. Then there's the sad tale about the two story house. The real estate man told him one story before he bought it and another one afterward.

750. "There are advantages and disadvantages about this property," said the honest real estate agent.

"To the north is the gas works, to the east a glue factory, to the south a fish and chip shop, and to the west a sewage farm. Those are the disadvantages."

"What are the advantages?" asked the prospective buyer.

"You can always tell which way the wind is blowing," said the agent.

Reciprocation

751. In the ladies lounge of a big city hotel there's a pay turnstile between the lounge and the lavatory. Four matrons were searching for change when one of them said: "No, Myrtle, you took us to lunch. This is my treat."

752. Mr. Jackson and his wife were playing golf. Mr. Jackson's first tee shot sliced across the fairway and hit the wife of another man out golfing.

The second husband stormed over to Mr. Jackson. "Do you know what you did?" he shouted. "You hit my wife with your ball!"

"Sorry," said Mr. Jackson, handing him a ball. "Have a shot at mine."

753. A very poor Chinese operated a small laundry next door to a more prosperous Chinese restaurant. Every day he would take his simple bowl of rice, place his chair as near as he dared to the restaurant, and sniff the appetizing aromas as he ate.

One day, he received a bill from his neighbor "for smell of food." He went into his laundry and came out with his tiny money box. This he rattled in the ears of his creditor, saying, "I hereby pay for the smell of your food with the sound of my money."

Resourcefulness

754. A practical medical school in Switzerland gives each graduating student a batch of ten-year-old copies of *Life* magazine—so patients won't think they are new in the business.

755. "Didn't I hear the clock strike two as you came in last night?" asked the wife at the breakfast table.

"Yes, dear," her spouse replied sweetly from behind the morning paper. "It started to strike ten but I stopped it to keep from waking you."

756. As a woman approached her car in a crowded parking lot, a policeman stopped her. "Your license plates are on upside down!" he exclaimed. "I know," she explained brightly. "It saves me a lot of time. Now I don't have to wander over the whole lot looking for my car."

757. The wife of a prominent Englishman constantly declared that upon his death she would dance on his grave; and she repeated the jibe regularly throughout recurring attacks the poor man suffered, including his last. But in expiration he foiled her plan, for contained in his will was an irrevocable legal codicil directing that he be buried at sea.

758. A motorist overtook a young man running along the road. He stopped his car and asked the perspiring runner to get in.

"An emergency, I gather?" the driver asked.

"No," puffed the young man. "I always run like that when I want a ride. It seldom fails."

759. A young mother was worried about her nine-year-old son. No matter how much she scolded, he kept running around with his shirt tails flapping. On the other hand, her neighbor had four boys, and each of them always wore his shirt neatly tucked in. Finally, in desperation the young mother asked her neighbor to tell her the secret.

"Oh, it's all very simple," she replied. "I just take all their shirts and sew an edging of lace on the bottom."

760. Timmy had only two pennies in his pocket when he approached the farmer and pointed to a tomato hanging lusciously from a vine.

"Give you two cents for it," the boy offered.

"That kind brings a nickel," the farmer told him.

"This one?" Timmy asked, pointing to a smaller, greener and less tempting specimen. The farmer nodded agreement. "Okay," said Timmy, and sealed the deal by placing his two pennies in the farmer's hand. "I'll pick it up in about a week."

761. A famed explorer was captured by savages in the wilds of South America. They were dancing around him in preparation for the kill when an idea struck the explorer—he would awe them with "magic." From his pocket he took a cigarette lighter.

"See," he said, "I am a fire-maker!" And with a flick of his thumb, the lighter burst into flame. The savages fell back in astonishment.

"Magic!" cried the explorer in triumph.

"Sure is," replied the chief. "Only time we ever saw a lighter work the first time."

762. Here's a suggestion for parents who become naturally worried when their youngsters who are away from home, either at camp or college, and who neglect to write:

Just send the boy your usual letter and then add a postscript something like this: "Hope you can use the $10 I am enclosing." Then don't enclose it.

The boy may not have written home for a long time, but that appended message will bring a letter in a hurry. And he'll be sure to add his own little worried postscript. "I didn't find the $10 you mentioned."

763. A small truck loaded with glassware backed out of a factory driveway into the path of a large truck. Most of the glass was broken in the crash, and the driver seemed on the verge of tears. A big crowd gathered, and one benevolent old gentleman said compassionately:

"I suppose you will have to make this good out of your own pocket?"

"I'm afraid so," lamented the driver.

"Well, well," said the gentleman. "Here's a dollar for you. Let me pass your hat and I dare say some of these kind people will help you out, too."

Over a hundred people dropped bills into the outstretched hat. The driver, stowing the money away as the crowd dispersed, nodded toward the retreating back of the benevolent old gentleman.

"That's what I call a smart guy—he's my boss."

764. A rabbi and two friends, one a Protestant minister, and the other a Catholic priest, played three-handed cards for small stakes one night a week. Nothing wrong with that except they lived in a small blue-law town. The sheriff raided their game and brought all three before a justice of the peace, who after listening to the sheriff's story, sternly asked the priest:

"Were you gambling, Father?"

The priest looked heavenward, whispered, "Oh Lord, forgive me," then said aloud to the JP:

"No, your Honor, I was not gambling."

"Were you gambling, Reverend?" the JP asked the Protestant minister, who, like the priest, also looked upward and whispered for forgiveness before he answered the JP:

"No, your Honor, I was not gambling."

The JP addressed the third clergyman:

"Were you gambling, Rabbi?"

Looking the JP squarely in the eye, the rabbi shrugged and replied:

"With whom?"

Restaurant—Restaurants

765. *Waitress:* "We have practically everything on the menu."

Patron: "So I see. Can you bring me a clean one?"

766. The man sawed on his steak, and he jabbed it, but still he couldn't cut it. He called the waiter.

The waiter examined the steak. "Sorry, I can't take it back," he said. "You've already bent it."

767. The proprietor called his waitresses together and said: "Girls, I want you to look your best today. Give these doctors a big smile. Kid them a little, serve them quickly and get out of the way."

"What's the matter?" asked one waitress. "They having a special program?"

"Nope," replied the owner. "The beef's tough again."

768. The clock in a restaurant window had stopped a few minutes past noon. One day a friend asked the owner if he knew the clock was not running. "Yes," replied the restaurant man, "but you would be surprised to know how many people look at that clock, think they are hungry, and come in to get something to eat."

769. The customer in the cafe had been waiting unattended for twenty minutes and finally, his patience exhausted, he called after a passing waitress: "Hi, Miss—can I see your manager —I have a complaint."

"Complaint," she said haughtily, eyeing him up and down. "This is a cafe, not a nursing home."

770. She was one of those fussy women who sometimes come into a restaurant. "Now mind you," she said, "I want my egg fried exactly 1½ minutes. The white part should be done real nice but I don't want the yolk to get too hard. About half a pinch of salt . . . no more, no less. A sniff of pepper. Oh, yes, make sure the frying pan isn't too greasy. And I like my eggs straight from the country."

"One thing, lady," said the waitress ever so sweetly. "The hen's name is Doris. Is that all right?"

Retirement

771. *Retiree:* "Age is a matter of attitude. I'm retreaded, not retired."

772. A letter of resignation from a woman who had quit to have a baby, said: "Dear Boss: I am getting too big for this job . . ."

773. And then there is the story of the gentleman who, when asked why he only wore the tops of his pajamas, replied: "Well, you see, I'm semi-retired."

Reunion, Class

774. After returning from his 50th college reunion at a large midwestern university, the father told his son that it had been different from other reunions. "Why?" he asked.

"Well," he answered, "at the 50th reunion they put the men and women up in the same dormitories."

775. All day long Mrs. Smith's maid had gone around red-eyed and moping. Finally Mrs. Smith could stand it no longer. "For heaven's sake, Mary," she exclaimed, "what is the matter?"

"I—don't know how to tell you, ma'am," sobbed the maid, "but I overheard Mr. Smith talking on the telephone. And . . . Oh, ma'am. He said it in so many words. He's packing up and going back to his old girl friend this weekend."

"His old girl friend?" Mrs. Smith, though excited and suddenly suspicious, kept control. "He didn't happen to mention her name, did he, Mary?"

"That he did," said Mary, proudly. "And I got it, all right, Alma Mater."

Romance

776. A woman might as well propose; her husband will claim she did.

777. A girl strings along with a guy only to see if he's fit to be tied.

778. Is it better to have loved and lost or to have won and be bossed?

779. Lots of girls can be had for a song. Trouble is, it's the wedding march.

780. Many a woman has started out playing with fire and has ended up cooking over it.

781. "Four long years of college," sighed the girl graduate, "and who has it got me?"

782. An unmarried girl is like a baseball player—always trying to turn a single into a double.

783. She didn't want to marry him for his money, but she just couldn't figure out any other way to get it.

784. *Advice to single gals:* Don't go looking for the ideal man, a husband is much easier to find.

785. There once was a botanist who crossed an intersection with a convertible and got a blonde.

786. *Blonde to boy friend at marriage-license bureau:* "Seems sort of silly to get a license after the hunting is over."

787. "Just give me my golf, the great outdoors, and a beautiful girl . . . and you can keep my golf and the great outdoors."

788. The girl who works does not ruin her chances of getting a husband . . . especially a girl who works fast.

789. The only difference in the game of love over the last few thousand years is that they've changed trumps from clubs to diamonds.

790. The trouble with many girls these days is that too often they look for a man smart enough to make lots of money but stupid enough to give most of it to them.

791. "The time will come," says a sociologist, "when girls will take the initiative in making proposals." And some of these days birds will learn how to fly.

792. A Hollywood starlet had just broken off her engagement to her wealthy fiance. "I saw him in a swim suit one day," she explained, "and he looked so different without his wallet."

793. "When I was a single girl," she said reflectively, "I said I would never marry a man who was bald, wore glasses or had artificial teeth. I didn't—but now he is, does, and has!"

794. There are two ways of achieving success: By putting your shoulder to the wheel or putting your head on the shoulder of the man at the wheel.

795. *Doris:* "When is your sister, Alice Ann, thinking of getting married?"
Little brother: "Constantly."

796. Accidentally meeting an acquaintance after several years, a girl said, "I never imagined you'd marry the man you did."
"Neither did I," replied the other. "I disliked his ways but I adored his means."

797. "I spent $20,000 on my daughter's education, and you want to marry her on an income of $1,000 a year!"
"Well, sir, that's five per cent on your investment."

798. *Father:* "So you want to become my son-in-law, do you?"
Suitor: "No, sir, I really don't. But I want to marry your daughter so I don't see how I can avoid it."

799. *Father:* "Jane, is that young man who is hanging around here so much really serious in his intentions?"

Daughter: "He must be. He wants to know how much I make, what kind of meals Mom serves, and if you two are easy to get along with."

800. The playful, middle-aged wolf sidled up to the brunette. "Where have you been all my life?" he asked.

She looked at him coolly and replied: "Well for the first half of it, I wasn't born!"

801. "Mother," said the teenage daughter, "what's the name of the boy I met on my vacation?"

"Which one, dear?" mother asked.

"You know, the one I couldn't live without."

802. One convict told his cellmate that a very nice thing had happened in the prison in which they were inmates—the warden's daughter had just married one of the cons who was serving a life term. And the warden was a little upset—because they had eloped.

803. "We are going to have a swell time tonight," the boy friend suggested. "I've got three seats for the theatre."

"Why do we need three seats?" she asked.

"They're for your father, mother, and kid brother," he said.

804. A curvacious cutie gave up her job as a secretary to marry an oil man.

"He's the man I've always dreamed would one day come along and win me," she confided to her girl friends. "He's tall, dark—and has some."

805. The young man was rather shy, and after she had thrown her arms around him and kissed him for bringing her a bouquet of flowers, he jumped up and grabbed his hat.

"Oh, don't go," she said, as he made for the door. "I didn't mean to offend you."

"Oh, I'm not offended," he replied. "I'm going for more flowers."

806. A man who had been keeping company with a girl for several years took her to a Chinese restaurant. Studying the menu, he asked, "How would you like your rice—fried or boiled?"

Looking him straight in the eye, she replied, "Thrown."

807. Shirley was racing around the porch with the neighbor's son close at her heels.

"Why are you chasing her?" Shirley's father asked.

"She pinched me," he replied.

Father turned to Shirley. "Why did you pinch him?"

Blushing prettily she whispered to her father, "So he would chase me."

808. A young prep-school lad is trying to decipher the following letter from his current girl friend: "Dear John, I hope you are not still angry. I want to explain that I was really joking when I told you I didn't mean what I said about reconsidering my decision not to change my mind. Please believe I really mean this. Love, Grace."

809. Stressing the importance of a large vocabulary, the English teacher told his class, "Use a word ten times and it will be yours for life."

In the back of the room a pert blonde closed her eyes and was heard chanting under her breath: "Fred, Fred, Fred, Fred, Fred, Fred, Fred, Fred, Fred, Fred."

810. "Why is it that you go steady with the girl?"

"Well, because she's different from other girls, I guess."

"How's that? In what way is she different?"

"She'll go with me."

811. She suddenly had an urge to live in the past. "You

used to kiss me." So he leaned over and kissed her. "You used to hold my hand." So he reached out and held her hand. "You used to bite me on the back of the neck." He got up and walked out of the room.

"Where are you going?"

"To get my teeth."

812. "Thought you were going to visit that blonde in her apartment tonight."

"I did."

"How come then you're home so early?"

"Well, we sat awhile and chatted. Then, suddenly, she turned out the lights. I can take a hint."

813. It was a family summer scene—a pretty young woman sitting on her porch knitting tiny garments while her mother gardened nearby.

A neighbor passing by was visibly touched by the tableau.

"My, Mrs. Frisbee," she exclaimed. "It's nice to see Alice so relaxed and domesticated."

"Isn't it?" answered the mother. "I'm so delighted she has taken an interest in something besides running around with boys!"

S

Safety first

814. Flying to Los Angeles from San Francisco the other day, a passenger noticed that the "Fasten Seat Belts" sign was kept lit during the whole journey although the flight was a particularly smooth one.

Just before landing, he asked the stewardess about it.

"Well," explained the girl, "up front there are 17 University of California girls going to Los Angeles for the weekend. In back, there are 25 Coast Guard enlistees. What would you do?"

815. A man phoned the local fire station one night and asked, "Is this the Fire Department?"

"Yes," he was told.

"Listen," said the man. "I've just moved here, and I've spent a lot on the garden. I engaged men to . . ."

"Where's the fire?" interrupted the officer at the station.

". . . dig out the old stuff and lay out new lawns and beds. The lawn alone set me back . . ."

"Is your house on fire?" yelled the officer.

"No," the man said, "but the one next door is, and if anybody gets in touch with you about it, I don't want clodhoppin' firemen draggin' hoses all over my new garden, see?"

Salary. See Wages

Salesmanship

816. A high-pressured auto salesman told his customer, "Do you realize that, while you're standing here dickering, your car is depreciating?"

817. A shoe salesman who had dragged out half his stock to a woman customer, said: "Mind if I rest a few minutes, lady? Your feet are killing me!"

818. There's nothing quite as pathetic looking in a hotel dining room as a salesman with an unlimited expense account and with ulcers.

819. *Customer:* "To what do you owe your extraordinary success as a house-to-house salesman?"
Salesman: "To the first five words I utter when a woman opens the door: 'Miss, is your mother in?' "

820. The new sales manager had called the sales force together and was laying down the law. "There's going to be a new regime around here—all work. And," he concluded, "from now on, I want you out of here and calling on your customers at the stroke of 9."
The salesman next to me, always the wise guy, piped up, "The first stroke of 9 or the last stroke, sir?"

821. A persistent salesman refused to leave when the secretary told him the boss was out. An hour passed, then two. Finally, weary of being a prisoner in his own office, the boss admitted the salesman.

"My secretary told you I was out," exclaimed the puzzled boss. "How'd you know I was in?"

"Easy," explained the salesman. "Your secretary was working."

822. Marshall Field, the merchant prince, once chided one of his department heads for stocking a fine Italian tablecloth. "You will never sell that in Chicago," he forecast.

A few weeks later the merchant dropped by to see his executive. "Barton," he said, "I owe you an apology. You did sell that tablecloth; I dined from it last night in a north side home."

"Yes," agreed the department head, "but your hostess returned it this morning for credit."

823. A second-hand car dealer having made a quick sale earlier was alarmed to see the purchaser driving back into his yard.

"Nothing wrong is there?"

"Not yet—I just wanted to return some things the previous owner, that quiet little titled lady, left in the car—her tobacco pouch in the glove locker and a bottle of Scotch under the seat!"

824. The salesman's knock was answered by something beautiful.

"Oh, good morning madam. May I speak to your husband?"

"Sorry, he's away on business, and won't be back for a week."

He took another long look, sighed, and asked: "May I come in and wait?"

825. An itinerant salesman for a children's encyclopedia was concluding a highly-charged sales talk. As the young mother hesitated, he turned to her five-year-old son and said, "Ask me a question, sonny. Ask me anything you want to know and I will show your mother where she can find the answer in this wonderful book."

The salesman is working on another street now. The question the boy asked was, "What kind of a car does God drive?"

826. A small businessman was in trouble with his sales. He decided to call in an expert to give him an outsider's viewpoint. After he had gone over his plans and problems, the businessman took the sales expert to a map on the wall and showed him brightly colored pins stuck wherever he had a salesman.

"Now," he asked the expert, "for a starter, what is the first thing we should do?"

"Well," replied the expert, "the first thing is to take those pins out of the map and stick them in the salesmen."

827. The sales manager was praising the efficiency of his organization at a banquet.

"We're now making a sale every three minutes," he announced proudly.

"That's not enough," came a voice from the audience.

The speaker paid no attention to the rude interruption but went on to tell of the new sales promotion and direct-mail campaign which would insure a sale every minute and a half.

"That's still not enough," the voice repeated.

Enraged, the speaker singled out the man who had spoken and barked, "You interrupted me twice. Now I wish you'd explain your remark."

"Certainly," came the reply, "there's a sucker born every minute."

828. A sportsman rented a dog at a hunting lodge and had wonderful luck with him. A month later he went back and described the dog he wanted because he had forgotten to ask its name.

"Oh, you want Salesman," beamed the lodge owner. "We've raised his rate from $5.00 to $10.00."

The sportsman took the dog out anyway and enjoyed another fine day. When he went back the following month, he asked for Salesman. The lodge owner explained that the dog was now called "Super-Salesman" and cost $15. The sportsman took him out just the same, insisting he was well worth the money.

The next month when the sportsman drove up in his car, the lodge owner greeted him with a sad smile. He said, "You can't have your favorite dog this time. A few days ago we made the mistake of naming him 'Sales Manager.' Now, all he will do is sit on his tail and bark."

829. An insurance salesman was called on by the president of the company to report on the technique he used to sell a one million dollar policy.

"Men," the ace began, "I followed the rule book. When I got to his office, knowing what sticklers doctors are, I made sure to arrive on the button for our appointment. But the place was jammed. I waited four hours to see him, and he appreciated it. He told me that it was a pleasure to meet a salesman who knows how to conduct himself in a professional man's office. I smiled, warmly, let him know that it was quite all right, and used this cue to ask him about himself. I listened attentively to every word, going out of my way to agree with the wonderful opinion he had of himself. He talked three hours, then asked me to come back. I did the next week, went through the same procedures, made the sale, and when I left his office I knew I'd made a friend for life." Then, after a pause, he concluded: "But boy! ! What an enemy *he* made."

830. Uncle Joe Cannon, once the czar-like Speaker of the House of Representatives, announced one summer that he would take a party of friends through Yellowstone National Park. That was the opportunity for which Hiram Martin Chittenden had been waiting. Mr. Chittenden was the builder of the park road system.

There were four stagecoaches ready for Uncle Joe and his party. When the guests turned up, Chittenden arranged to have

Uncle Joe placed in the last coach. The driver was instructed to keep as close to the coach ahead as he could without inviting disaster.

What a powdering Uncle Joe took back there! He was white with volcanic dust.

"Why in the devil," he rasped, "doesn't somebody do something about those blankety-blank roads?"

Chittenden, in a gentle voice, reminded him that there were plans drawn up but that there was no money available.

"Well, let's see the plans," ordered Mr. Cannon.

And out of the next Congress came $350,000 for the next three years, 1902-1905.

Season—Seasons

831. Have you heard about the playboy who winters in Florida, summers in Maine, falls for women and springs at blondes?

832. "The weather here in Florida is wonderful," said the old lady. "How do you tell summer from winter?"

Replied the hotel clerk: "In winter we get Cadillacs, Lincolns and stuffed shirts. In summer we get Chevrolets, Fords and stuffed shorts."

Secrecy

833. "What is the difference between a secret and a public session of the town council?"

"When there is a secret session, one knows the result an hour later; the result of a public session, one reads in the next day's paper."

Secretary—Secretaries

834. *Advice to office girls:* "Take your shorthand at arm's length."

835. After a boss' wife discovers he's got a beautiful secretary, he usually becomes shorthanded.

Self-confidence

836. A college professor, telling a student that there was no excuse for his poor spelling, said: "You should consult a dictionary whenever you are in doubt. It's as simple as that."

The student appeared confused. "But, sir," he replied, "I'm never in doubt."

837. While stopping at a New England hotel, a high-pressured New York executive was suddenly taken ill. The elderly physician who attended him was much too deliberate for his taste. "Don't know why I'm letting you take care of me in the first place," snapped the executive. "Guess I just have a lot of faith in fools."

"Yup," replied the old country doctor agreeably. "I can see you have a remarkable amount of self-confidence."

838. In his younger days, French statesman Georges Clemenceau fought a number of duels.

On one occasion, he was to fight a duel in a suburb of Paris. He went with his second to the railway station and bought a one-way ticket.

"A one-way ticket?" said the second. "Pessimistic?"

"Not at all," said Clemenceau cheerfully. "I always use my opponent's return ticket for the trip back."

Self-love

839. Israel Zangwill once remarked about the great George Bernard Shaw: "The way Shaw believes in himself is very refreshing in these atheistic days when so many believe in no God at all."

Semantics

840. *Bishop (reading telegram from one of his ministers)*: "My wife passed away Wednesday. Please send substitute for over the weekend."

Sharing

841. The bus was already crowded when the fat woman entered. She stood for a moment glaring at the seated passengers. "Isn't some gentleman going to offer me a seat" she asked.

At this, one exceptionally small man rose. "Well," he said, rather shyly, "I'm willing to make a contribution."

842. *Wife:* "Is it true that money talks?"
Husband: "That's what they say."
Wife: "Well, leave a little here to talk to me today. I get so lonely."

Silence

843. One way to save face is to keep the lower half shut.

844. "Your boy friend stayed very late last night, didn't he?"

"Yes, mother, did the noise disturb you?"
"No, but the periods of silence did."

845. At a dinner party, the subject of eternal life and future punishment came up for a lengthy discussion.

Mark Twain took no part in it, so the woman seated next to him asked: "Why haven't you said something? Surely you must have some opinion about this."

"Madam, you must excuse me," Twain replied. "I am silent because of necessity. I have friends in both places."

846. The story is told that when Western Union offered to buy the ticker invented by Thomas Edison, the great inventor was unable to name a price. Edison asked for a couple of days to consider it. Talking the matter over with his wife, she suggested he ask $20,000, but this seemed exorbitant to Edison. At the appointed time, Edison returned to the Western Union office. He was asked to name his price. "How much?" asked the Western Union official. Edison tried to say $20,000, but lacked the courage, and just stood there speechless.

The official waited a moment, then broke the silence and said, "Well, how about $100,000?"

Sin

847. A preacher recently announced that there are 726 different kinds of sin. He is now being besieged with requests for the list, mostly from people who think they are missing something.

848. The pastor was rejoicing with a little old lady over one of her elderly relatives, who had finally seen the light and joined the church after a lifetime of riotous living.

When she wondered if all the oldster's carryings-on would be forgiven, the pastor assured her, "Yes, indeed, the greater the sinner, the greater the saint."

"Preacher," she mused wistfully. "I wish I had learned this forty years ago."

Size

849. George Washington Carver, Negro scientist who achieved wonders with the humble peanut, used to tell this story:

When I was young I said to God, "God, tell me the mystery of the universe." But God answered, "That knowledge is reserved for Me alone." So I said, "God tell me the mystery of the peanut." Then God said, "Well, George, that's more nearly your size." And He told me.

850. A man walked into a pet shop, pointed to a large dog in a kennel and said:

"How much do you want for that big dog?"

"Fifty dollars," replied the clerk.

"And how much for that small fellow over there?" asked the customer.

"One hundred dollars," was the reply.

"And for that tiny one?"

"Two hundred dollars," said the clerk.

The customer looked puzzled.

"How much," he asked, "will it cost me if I don't buy a dog at all?"

Smoking

851. "Sir," said the intrusive lady to a stranger seated next to her on the train, "smoking makes me sick."

"Well, then, madam," replied the stranger, "if I were you I'd give it up."

852. On her son's seventeenth birthday a mother pleadingly asked, "Promise me you'll tell me when you start smoking. Don't let me find it out from the neighbors."

"Don't worry about me, Mom," the son replied. "I quit smoking a year ago."

853. The visitor turned to the hostess and said, "My, this is a fancy vase on your mantel. What's this in it?"

"My husband's ashes," she replied.

"Oh, I'm sorry," said the visitor. "How long has he been dead?"

"Oh, he's not dead," said the wife. "He's just too lazy to find an ashtray."

854. A young preacher came to one of the distant settlements and started in to reform the natives. Among other things to which he objected was smoking by women. He stopped one day at Old Nancy's cabin and found her enjoying an after-dinner smoke on her corncob pipe.

"Aunt Nancy," he said, "when your time comes to go and you apply for admission at the gate of Heaven, do you expect that St. Peter will let you in if he detects the odor of tobacco on your breath?"

The old woman took the pipe out of her mouth and said: "Young man, when I go to Heaven I expect to leave my breath behind."

Space, Outer. See Outer space

Specialization

855. *Fair maid:* "Why, sir, what kind of a doctor are you?"
Officer: "I'm a naval surgeon."
Fair maid: "Goodness, how you doctors do specialize."

Spelling

856. *School term report card:* "Your son's handwriting is so bad we cannot tell whether he can spell or not."

857. The nice thing about dictating letters is that you can use a lot of words you don't know how to spell.

858. *Secretary:* "Sometimes I think our boss is a jerk. He told me to cross one of the 't's' out of 'rabbitt' but didn't say which one."

859. *Daughter:* "Oh, mother, I took Henry into the loving room last night and . . ."
Mother: "That's *living*, dear . . ."
Daughter: "You're telling me."

860. The examination question was a real puzzler. It asked why "psychic" is spelled with a "p".
The young student in the far corner did not have the answer, but he felt he should not leave the question unheeded. Shaking his head, he wrote, "It pcertainly does pseem psilly."

861. "I think," said the dizzy typist to her friend, "that the boss has decided to keep me."
"Has he said anything?"
"No. But this morning he gave me a dictionary."

862. A man picked up the phone and asked for the telegraph office. His connection was completed and he told the clerk: "I want to send a telegram to Pottawatomie, Indiana."
"Please spell it," the clerk said.
"Listen, lady," the man said, "if I could spell it, I wouldn't send a telegram—I'd write a letter."

Sports

863. She would be terrific in the Olympics. She can hang over a bar and chin for hours.

864. From a report of the American Psychological Association: "Women who are cooperative and good sports are more likely to have big families."

865. Just as the trio of baseball umpires was walking onto the field before a big crowd, the band struck up the embarrassing tune, "Three Blind Mice."

866. A Russian track coach, interviewed by an American sportswriter, was asked why the Soviets are now producing such fast runners.

"It's really quite simple," the coach replied. "We use real bullets in our starting guns."

867. A glamorous movie star was guest of honor at a football coaches' luncheon one day.

She made a clever little talk which ended with the remark, "I probably have devised more defensive plays than the whole lot of you put together."

868. Two old ladies decided to take in one of the bowl games on New Year's Day. They watched the kickoff and the various plays throughout a scoreless first half.

When the teams lined up for the second-half kickoff, one of them turned to the other and said, "It's time to go home. This is where we came in."

869. A minister walked through the lobby of a hotel one morning and noticed a ballplayer he knew by sight. So he sauntered over to the player and introduced himself and said: "One thing I've always wondered. Why must you play ball on Sunday?"

"Well, Reverend," smiled the player, "Sunday is our biggest day—we get the best crowds—take in more money—and after all, Sunday is your biggest day, too, isn't it?"

There was a nod of understanding, but the minister explained: "But there's a little difference. You see, I'm in the right field." The player brightened and responded eagerly: "So am I, and ain't the sun hell out there?"

Status quo

870. A woebegone-looking adventurer reached the riverside, and approached the old boatman who operated the ferry across the stream. "Dad," he whined, "I'm broke and have to get across the river. Will you trust me for it?"

"Fare's only a quarter," said the ferryman.

"I know it, but I haven't got a nickel," explained the traveler.

The old boatman took a puff at his pipe. "Well, mister," he said, "if you ain't got a nickel you won't be no better off on the other side than you are here."

Stinginess

871. "Did you read in the paper where old Andy McAndrews has left a quarter of a million dollars?"

"That old miser didn't leave a penny! He was *separated* from it."

Surprise

872. "I told her I wanted to be surprised for dinner, so she soaked the labels off the cans."

873. The lady in the bathtub heard a knock at the front door.

"Who's there?" she called out.

"A blind salesman," came the answer.

Thinking it would be entirely proper, she went to the door as she was. A young man stepped inside with: "Here's the blinds you ordered. Where shall I put 'em?"

874. A middle-aged man set off for a house where a children's party had been arranged. "Don't announce me," he said to the man who let him in.

Leaving his hat and coat in the hall, he opened the drawing-room door, through which a buzz of conversation could be heard. Dropping on his hands and knees, he entered making noises like a horse neighing.

There was a dead silence. He looked up and found half a dozen people regarding him with perplexity and alarm. He was in the wrong house.

Suspense

875. A film actor took his wife to the hospital for the birth of their first child. For the purpose of the film on which he had been working, the father-to-be sported a two-weeks' growth of very dark beard. While waiting anxiously, he was joined by another expectant father—a haggard young man who paced the floor for several minutes before noticing the first man sitting in a corner. When he did spot him, the young man turned pale.

"Good heavens!" he said. "How long have you been waiting?"

Suspicion

876. Did you hear about the wife who cured her husband of his "have to work late at the office" routine? She asked him if she could depend upon it.

877. "Your husband looks like a brilliant man—I'll bet he knows everything."

"Don't be silly—he doesn't suspect a thing."

878. Interviewing a woman applicant, a kindly Social Security claims representative wanted to make sure that no tangles would prevent her from getting her full benefits. "Were either you or your husband married before?" he asked.

The woman glared indignantly and snapped: "Before what?"

879. "I don't like to pry into your affairs," said the lady to her husband. "But something's been bothering me for days."

"So?" said the husband. "Tell me all about it."

"You got a letter last Friday," the lady said. "It was perfumed. It was in a girl's handwriting. I saw you open it; you broke into a sweat. You turned white. Your hands trembled . . . For goodness' sake, who was it from and what did it say?"

"Oh, that," said the husband. "I decided it was best for both of us not to talk about it at the time. I've been trying to think of the best way of discussing it with you without causing an explosion."

"For heaven's sake," screamed the woman. "Tell me who it was from and what it said."

"Okay," said the husband. "It was from your dress shop. It said you owe them $740.00."

T

Table-turning

880. *Patient to dentist:* "This may hurt a little. I don't have the money."

881. Henry Ward Beecher, famous New England clergyman, was opening his mail one morning. Drawing a single sheet of paper from an envelope, he found written on it the one word: *Fool.*

The next Sunday, in the course of his sermon, he referred to it in these words: "I have known many an instance of a man writing letters and forgetting to sign his name. But this is the only instance I've ever known of a man signing his name and forgetting to write his letter."

Tact

882. When a prominent clergyman was asked his opinion of advertising in America, he hesitated to make any comment on advertising itself, but he did offer to pray for the people who made a living at it.

883. Georges Clemenceau, noted French statesman, was in the habit of bluntly speaking his mind, to the dismay of his political advisers.

"You must be more tactful," they urged him. "Your strong language only makes you enemies."

Clemenceau couldn't see it that way.

"It also makes me friends," he argued. "I have as my supporters all the enemies of my enemies."

884. The captain approached the sergeant with a bit of bad news. "Sergeant," he said, "we just got notice that Smith's grandmother died. You'd better go break the news to him."

The sergeant walked into the barracks, paused at the doorway and shouted, "Hey, Smith, your grandmother died."

The captain was horrified. "Sergeant, that's no way to tell a man that his grandmother has died. Look how you've shocked him. You have to use tact in a situation like this. I think we'd better send you to Tact and Diplomacy School."

So the sergeant spent a year studying at Tact and Diplomacy School. On the day he returned, the captain approached him.

"Well, sergeant, how did you do in school?"

"Fine," replied the sergeant. "I've really learned how to be tactful."

"That's good, because we've just gotten notice that Lopez's grandmother died. Go in and tell him."

The sergeant entered the barracks, paused at the doorway and called his men to attention. When they were lined up he stepped before them and ordered, "All those with living grandmothers step forward. Not so fast, Lopez."

Talkativeness. See Loquacity

Tardiness

885. Widows are not the only people who have late husbands.

886. Husbands have always had a leisure problem It's called waiting.

887. *Steno to irate boss:* "Certainly I have a good reason for being late! It makes the day seem shorter!"

888. *Boss:* "You're twenty-five minutes late, young man. Don't you know what time our people start to work around here?"
Office boy: "No, sir. They're always at it when I get here."

Taxation

889. Taxation, like a lot of other things, is based on supply and demand. The Government demands, and we supply.

890. A pretty lass in a night-school English class was disturbed when the instructor announced: "Tomorrow night we will take up syntax."
"Goodness!" she exclaimed. "If they're going to collect *that*, I'll never be able to afford the tuition."

Taxes

891. There's this to be said about taxes—if the taxpayer is alive, he's kicking.

892. *This sign on a New York service station:* "We collect taxes—federal, state, and local. We also sell gasoline as a sideline."

893. The biggest job Congress has is how to get the money from the taxpayer without disturbing the voter.

894. Two men were discussing the high rate of taxes and government waste of money. Just then a school bus passed them. "See what I mean," exclaimed one. "When I was a boy we walked three miles to school and three miles back home each day. Now we spend $5,000 for a bus to pick up the children so they don't have to walk. Then we spend $50,000 for a gymnasium so they can get exercise."

895. Once, when William Gladstone was Britain's Chancellor of the Exchequer, he attended a lecture given by Michael Faraday, the physicist. When it was over, Gladstone said to the scientist: "What you spoke about is purely theoretical, but does it have any practical value?"

"What do you mean by 'practical value'?" asked Faraday.

"I mean," replied Gladstone, "can it be taxed?"

Teacher—Teaching

896. "How long do you plan to teach school?" the dean asked the pretty young thing as he handed her a teaching certificate.

She replied with a shy smile: "From here to maternity."

Teacher—Pupil

897. Somebody has said that payola started when the first kid gave his teacher an apple.

898. *History teacher:* "Johnny, name the addresses we best remember Washington and Lincoln by."

Johnny: "Mount Vernon and Springfield."

899. "What did you do in school?" a mother asked her little boy when he returned from his first academic day.

"Nothing," the boy replied. "Some woman wanted to know how to spell 'cat', and I told her."

900. To stimulate her young pupils, a first-grade teacher arranged to take her class on an "educational tour" of a farmyard.

But one small boy saw right through her scheme. "Don't look, don't look!" he warned his buddy. "If we look we'll have to tell about it tomorrow!"

901. *Teacher* (*pointing at a deer in the zoo*): "Johnny, what is that?"

Johnny: "I don't know."

Teacher: "What does your mother call your father?"

Johnny: "Don't tell me that's a louse."

902. One day a teacher asked her first-graders what they did to help at home. They took turns giving such answers as, "I dry dishes," "I feed the dog," and "I make my bed." Then she noticed that Johnny hadn't spoken, so she asked him to tell what he did.

After hesitating a moment, he replied: "Mostly, I stay out of the way."

903. *Teacher:* "Which is more important to us—the moon or the sun?"

Pupil: "The moon."

Teacher: "Why?"

Pupil: "The moon gives us light at night when we need it. The sun gives us light only in the daytime when we don't need it."

904. *Teacher:* "Give me a sentence with an 'object' in it."

Pupil: "Teacher, you're the most wonderful and beautiful lady I've ever seen."

Teacher: "Thanks, but what's the 'object'?"

Pupil: "I'd like to go home a little earlier today."

905. "Now, how many of you would like to go to heaven?" asked the Sunday school teacher. All the eager three-year-olds raised their hands except Tommy.

"I'm sorry, I can't. My mother told me to come right home after Sunday school.'

Technique

906. How is it that a husband who bowls half the night without making a strike can manage to knock over all the milk bottles on the porch?

907. "Joe," a friend asked a young businessman, "how do you expect to accomplish anything at your office with three good-looking typists around?"

"Easy," was the confident answer. "I'll give two of them the same day off."

908. "Begin your story well," author Ian MacLaren once counseled a group of budding writers. "It's half the battle. Always bear in mind," he continued, "the case of the young man, who desiring to marry, obtained a favorable hearing from his sweetheart's father by opening the interview with the words: 'I know a way, sir, whereby you can save a lot of money.'"

Teenage

909. The teller at the deposit window of the bank sharply reprimanded a man because he had neither filled out a deposit slip nor put his loose silver in the special little rolls of specified amounts.

"When you've done this properly, I'll be glad to accept your deposit," said the teller curtly.

The man accepted this tirade meekly and went to a counter to follow instructions. When he returned later to the window the teller half-apologized.

"Oh, that's all right," said the man graciously. "I have a houseful of teenagers, so I'm used to being spoken to as if I were an idiot."

Telephone

910. The bathtub was invented in 1850, and the telephone in 1875. Had you lived in 1850, you could have sat in the bathtub for the next 25 years without having the phone ring once.

911. In the business world an executive knows something about everything, a technician knows everything about something—and the switchboard operator knows everything.

912. "Who was that on the telephone?" the man of the house asked his new maid.

"I dunno," she answered. "Someone just said, 'Long distance from New York.' So I said 'Yes, it certainly is' and hung up."

913. A telephone repairman, who had just installed some new equipment in the Pentagon, started to leave but became lost in the maze that has driven many a visitor to despair.

Finally, in a claustrophobic state, he ducked into an office and called to the girl at the switchboard:

"How in the devil do I get outside?"

"Just dial 9," snapped the girl busily.

914. "This is Perkins, Potter, Parker and Potts, good morning."

"Is Mr. Potter there?"

"May I ask who is calling?"

"This is Mr. Sullivan's office, of Sullivan, Chadwick, Bicknell and Jones."

"Just a moment, I'll connect you."

"Mr. Potter's office."

"Mr. Potter, please. Mr. Sullivan wants him."

"Will you put Mr. Sullivan on the line please."

"Mr. Sullivan? Ready with Mr. Potter."

"Hello, Pete? This is Joe. Okay for lunch? Good! See you."

Television

915. A lady phoned her TV serviceman and complained that something was wrong with her set. The serviceman asked her if there were any visible symptoms.

"The newscaster is on right now," said the lady, "and he has a very long face."

"Madam," replied the serviceman, "if you had to report what's happening these days you'd have a long face too."

916. A rating service learned that it inadvertently obtained part of its findings from prisoners in the same compound. They also discovered that the prisoners were only watching daytime TV.

Unable to resist its natural urge, the rating outfit asked the prisoners why they never watched at night.

"That's simple," explained a prisoner. "The lights go out at 8:00 and we are not allowed to watch after that."

"But why do you watch it during the daytime?" persisted the prober.

"I thought it was part of the punishment," replied the prisoner.

Theft

917. Some of us who talk too much at times may learn something from the mistake made by Rastus.

Judge: "Guilty, or not guilty?"

Rastus: "Not guilty, suh."

Judge: "Have you ever been in jail?"

Rastus: "No, suh, ah nevah stole nothin' befo'."

Thrift

918. The best thing to save for your old age is yourself.

919. The young couple walked into a car dealer's show-room and was taken aback by the suggested price of a compact car.

"But that's almost the cost of a big car," the husband said.

"Well," said the salesman, "if you want economy, you got to pay for it."

920. An old farmer was once asked by a young man how it was he had become so rich.

"It is a long story," said the old man, "and while I'm telling it we may as well save the candle." And he put it out.

"You need not tell the story," said the youth. "I understand."

921. A University of British Columbia professor who makes almost a ritual of walking to work, rain or shine, consented to accept a lift from a friend who overtook him hiking along through a heavier-than-usual coastal mist.

As the professor climbed in, the driver noticed he wore only one rubber and exclaimed sympathetically, "Lost a rubber, huh?" When the professor merely answered no, his friend demanded, "Isn't it a bit odd wearing only one?"

The professor said no again, adding, "Only one shoe has a hole in it."

Tip—Tips—Tipping

922. "I will take a meal out occasionally but I never get to the same restaurant twice," a man remarked. To which his friend quickly replied: "I don't ever leave a tip either."

923. *From Miami Beach:* "Bellboy, can I get change for a dollar?"

"Lady, at this hotel, a dollar is change."

924. "Your son tips me more generously than you do, sir," said the taxi driver.

"That's quite possible. He has a wealthy father. I haven't."

925. The homeowner was delighted with the way the painter had decorated his house.

"You did a fine job," he said, "and I'm going to give you a little something extra. Here's $10. Take the missus to a show."

That night the bell rang and the painter stood at the door, all dressed up.

"What is it," the man asked, "did you forget something?"

"No," replied the painter. "I just came to take the missus to a show."

926. The millionaire speculator, John W. (Bet-a-Million) Gates was a lavish tipper. Ironically, this resulted at times in poorer service.

Gates was a particular favorite of bellhops. At one time, when he was stopping at a New York hotel, he instructed his secretary to tip them 25¢ for any service, no matter how trivial.

After a few weeks, it struck him that he must be getting a staggering amount of service, as the tips were running into several hundred dollars a week. His heavy mail, about 100 letters a day, was being brought up with something less than promptness.

Gates put two and two together and made an investigation. Sure enough, he discovered that the mail was being delivered one letter at a time.

Tit for tat

927. *Man to neighbor:* "Let's make a deal. I'll stop keeping up with you, if you'll stop keeping up with me.'

211 ★ TIT FOR TAT

928. A wise teacher sent this note home at the start of the term: "If you promise not to believe everything your child says happens at school, I'll promise not to believe everything he says happens at home."

929. The wife was crying at her daughter's wedding. Her husband consoled her with the following: "Don't think of it as losing a daughter. Think of it as gaining a bathroom."

930. "I'm sorry if our hammering disturbed you. We were hanging a picture."

"Oh, that's perfectly all right. I just came over to ask if it was okay if we hung a picture on the other end of the nail."

931. A southern senator once pointed to a drove of mules just in from Ohio and said to Senator Tom Corwin: "There go some of your constituents."

"Yes," said the Ohio senator gravely. "They are on their way down South to teach school."

932. *John:* "My wife had an argument with the electric company."

Jim: "Who won?"

John: "It was a tie. We don't get any electricity, and they don't get any money."

933. "Dear Alice," wrote the young man, "I'm getting so forgetful, that while I remember proposing to you last night, I forgot whether you said 'Yes' or 'No'."

"Dear Bob," Alice replied, "so glad to hear from you. I knew I said 'No' to someone last night, but I had forgotten just who it was."

934. Parson Webster phoned the local board of health to ask that a dead mule be removed from in front of his house. The young clerk who answered thought he'd be smart.

"I thought you ministers took care of the dead," he wise-cracked.

"We do," answered the parson, "but first we get in touch with their relatives."

935. "How do you do, my dear?" said the old lady to the little girl.

"Quite well, thank you," was the polite reply.

There was a pause and then the old lady asked, "Why don't you ask me how I am?"

"Because," said the child calmly, "I'm not interested."

936. A native of Ireland applied for a job in a powder plant. "What can you do?" asked the foreman.

"Anything, sar, just anything," replied the hopeful man.

"Well," drawled the foreman, thinking to have some fun with the newcomer, "you seem to be all right. Could you wheel out a barrow of smoke?"

"Shure!" exclaimed the man. "Just fill it up for me!"

937. A lady phoned the president of a large department store at 2 a.m. After long ringing, a sleepy, gruff voice answered.

"This is Miss Gruntled," said the lady in sugary tones. "I just had to call you personally to tell you that the hat I bought at your store last week is simply stunning."

"I'm delighted to hear it," yawned the president. "But why, madam, why call me in the middle of the night about a hat you bought last week?"

"Because," she replied sweetly, "your truck just delivered it."

938. Two counterfeiters with a talented but stupid engraver found themselves with a large quantity of almost-perfect bills on their hands. The trouble was, they were all $18 bills. The crooks decided to go far back into the hill country to dispose of the bills because "nobody up there sees much money." Deep in the mountains, they flashed one on a crossroads storekeeper and talked him into changing it.

"How do you want it?" he asked. "Would two sevens and a four be all right?"

Traffic, Automobile

939. Some women have a wonderful sense of right and wrong, but little sense of right and left.

940. Air travel will be much safer when they eliminate the automobile ride between the city and the airport.

941. The automobile may have replaced the horse and buggy—but it's still wise for the drivers to stay on the wagon.

942. If you make a left turn from a right-hand lane, you are probably just careless or reckless and not at all what the driver behind called you.

Transformation, Religious

943. A party of clergymen were attending a Presbyterian conference in Scotland. Several of them set off to explore the district. Presently they came to a river spanned by a temporary bridge. Not seeing the notice that said it was unsafe, they began to cross it. The bridge keeper ran after them in protest.

"It is all right," declared the spokesman, not understanding the reason for the old man's haste, "we're Presbyterians from the conference."

"I'm no caring aboot that," was the reply, "but if ye dinna get off the bridge, you'll all be Baptists!"

Travel

944. There are only two ways to travel—first class and with children.

945. The best way to see America nowadays is to try to get your son, or daughter, into college.

946. People in big cities are not essentially rude. They are just afraid of being mistaken for visitors.

947. *Wife:* "I wish I could find a book to tell us where to go on a vacation this winter."
Husband: "We have one book to tell us where we can't go—our check book."

948. An American tourist stopped at an inn in a small French village and ordered a couple of scrambled eggs for lunch. Afterward he noted with astonishment that he had been charged a dollar apiece for them and asked, "Are eggs scarce here?"
"No, monsieur," said the innkeeper. "Eggs are plentiful. But Americans, they are scarce here."

949. A couple from New Haven, Connecticut, were driving through Maine in an attempt to discover their rich New England heritage.
When they stopped in front of the general store in a quaint old town, the visitor asked the proprietor what the town was noted for.
"Tourists," grunted the man sourly.
"But what do they raise here?"
The native eyed the young man with contempt and replied, "Hell."

Trouble—Troubles

950. People are like tea bags . . . they don't know their own strength until they get into hot water.

951. The wives of two prominent manufacturers were talking things over in the lobby of a hotel.

"Does your husband confide his business troubles to you?" asked one.

"Oh, yes, indeed," replied the other. "Every time I come home with a new dress!"

Truth

952. A piano manufacturer tried to get a testimonial from Will Rogers for his pianos. Rogers, who never endorsed any product unless he really believed in it, wrote this letter to the piano firm: "Dear Sirs: I guess your pianos are the best I ever leaned against. Yours truly, Will Rogers."

953. The wife of an art dealer, who was anxious to sell some Gothic tapestries to the great J. Pierpont Morgan, was amazed and annoyed when her husband awakened her at three o'clock one morning and commanded her to say, "I'll pay you a million dollars for your Gothic tapestries."

She could see no sense in that. In the first place, she didn't have a million dollars and even if she had, why should she offer to buy tapestries from her own husband?

"Just say it, please," he implored.

Sleepily she complied, repeated the suggested words, turned over and went back to sleep.

At nine o'clock the next morning the dealer, who took great pride in his integrity, told Mr. Morgan, "I can swear on a stack of Bibles that at three o'clock this morning I had an offer of a million dollars for those tapestries."

Turnabout

954. Then there was the one about the goose flying south for the winter who flew past a drive-in showing a horror movie and was so frightened he got people-pimples.

955. A Minneapolis man, convalescing after surgery, visited by his wife one evening, suggested a stroll. They wound up on the maternity floor, admiring the babies. While oohing and aahing, they heard muffled snickers, then realized the spectacle—the man in his hospital bathrobe, the woman in street clothes outside the nursery window.

956. Sam, the private eye, was giving his curvesome client a report. "I trailed your husband into four bars and then to a bachelor's apartment," he said.

"Aha!" exclaimed the wife. "Go on, go on! What was he doing there?"

"Well, lady," Sam responded in an embarrassed tone, "near as I could make out, he was trailing you."

Twins

957. An impetuous student negotiated a date with a pair of Siamese twins one night.

"Have a good time?" asked his roommate later.

"Yes and No."

958. Two young guys were discussing their conquests and the first young man reminisced rapturously about one of his former girl friends, mentioning that she was a twin.

"Twins?" his buddy queried. "How did you tell them apart?"

"Oh, that wasn't so hard. Her brother has a mustache!"

Vacation—Vacationing

959. "I need a vacation," said the pretty cashier. "I'm not looking my best."

"Nonsense," said the manager.

"It isn't nonsense, the men are beginning to count their change."

960. It was his first day back on the job after his vacation. "How did you enjoy your trip?" asked a fellow worker.

"Well," sighed the weary traveler, "have you ever spent four days in a station wagon with those you thought you loved best?"

961. One evening when Thomas Edison came home from work, his wife said to him, "You've worked long enough without a rest. You must go on a vacation."

"But where on earth would I go?" asked Mr. Edison.

"Just decide where you would rather be than anywhere else on earth," suggested the wife.

Mr. Edison hesitated. "Very well," he said finally, "I'll go to-morrow."

The next morning he was back at work in his laboratory.

Value—Values

962. A burglar gave his girl friend a fur coat. "It's wonderful," she exclaimed. "It must be worth at least ten years."

963. A family had just moved to a small town in New England and after finding a house to live in, the woman of the family was familiarizing herself with the local stores. Intent on getting some meat for her family's evening meal, she entered the only meat market in the village and was surprised to find only two trays of meat in the showcase. Upon closer examination she found that the meat looked exactly alike to her.

"How much is this meat?" she asked, pointing to one of the cases.

"Fifty cents a pound," replied the old butcher.

"And that?" she asked, pointing to the other tray.

"One dollar a pound," was his reply.

"What's the difference?" she asked.

"No difference," grunted the butcher. "Some people like to pay fifty cents a pound, some like to pay a dollar!"

Vocational aptitude

964. *Vocational advisor to youth:* "Your vocational aptitude test indicates that your best opportunities lie in a field where your father holds an influential position."

Vote—Votes—Voting

965. "Whom will your wife vote for?"
"She will vote as I vote."
"And whom will you vote for?"
"Well, I haven't talked it over with my wife yet.'

966. A farmer was detained for questioning about an elections scandal. "Did you sell your vote?" the U.S. Attorney asked.

"No sirree, not me," the farmer protested. "I voted for that there fella 'cause I liked him."

"C'mon, now," threatened the attorney. "I have good evidence that he gave you five dollars."

"Well, now," the farmer said, "it's plain common-sense that when a feller gives ya five dollars ya like him."

W

Wages

967. A shrewd gunman, who suddenly appeared at the paymaster's window of a large plant, demanded: "Never mind the payroll, Bud, just hand over the welfare fund, the group insurance premiums, the pension fund, and the withholding taxes."

968. One of the neatest ways of asking the boss for a raise in pay was the approach used by John Kieran when he was the sports columnist of the New York *Times*. Feeling the need for more dough but wanting to be tactful about it, Kieran went to his employer, Adolph Ochs, and said respectfully, "Mr. Ochs, working for the *Times* is a luxury I can no longer afford."

He got the raise.

969. A farmer, in great need of extra hands at haying time, finally asked Si Warren, a town character, if he could help him out.

"What'll ye pay?" asked Si.

"I'll pay what you're worth," replied the farmer.

Si scratched his head a minute, then said, "I won't work for that!"

970. A Nevadan, visiting New York for the first time, stopped a youngster on the street and offered him a dollar if he would show him the way to a certain bank. The boy complied, left the Westerner at the entrance to the bank, and stuck out his hand for the money.

The visitor reached for his wallet and commented that the boy had probably never earned a dollar that easily in all his life.

"Sure, mister," agreed the youngster, "but don't forget that us bank directors in New York is paid high!"

971. A company was having its annual dinner for the 25-year employees, and the boss had stepped up to the refreshment stand. A worker, fortified by a few trips to the same stand, decided now was the time to hit the old man for a raise.

So he walked over to the chief executive, stuck out his chin and stated bluntly:

"Mr. Jones, I've worked 25 years for you. I've worked so hard and so conscientiously I've ruined my health."

"I know you have, Smith," the boss answered, and raising his glass he said dramatically: "Here's to your health!"

Warning

972. "I'd like to bring Bill home to dinner tonight," the man telephoned his wife.

"To dinner tonight!" she screamed. "You idiot, you know that the cook just left, I've got a cold, baby's cutting his teeth, the furnace is broken and the butcher won't give us any more credit until we pay up . . ."

"I know," the husband interrupted quietly. "That's why I want to bring him. The poor fool is thinking of getting married."

973. The young minister was in the pulpit for the first time and he was a little nervous. He read the text: "Behold I Come." The sermon was to follow immediately, but his mind went blank, and he repeated the text: "Behold I Come," hoping to remember the opening words of the sermon—but with no success Trying to be nonchalant, he leaned forward as he repeated the text for the third time. Under his weight the pulpit gave way and he landed in the lap of the wife of one of the elders. "I'm awfully sorry," he said much embarrassed. "I really didn't mean for this to happen."

The lady smiled kindly and replied, "Oh, that's all right. I should have been ready after you warned me three times."

Wealth

974. The world might never have heard of Voltaire as a writer if he hadn't been a math whiz. Taking advantage of a government miscalculation in issuing a national lottery, he formed a syndicate and bought up every ticket. His share made him independent and gave him time to write. His success was assured by the Paris censors, who always banned his books and closed his plays.

975. A certain nobleman had a valet who was violently opposed to the capitalistic system, and who devoted most of his spare time to attending meetings where he could listen while communistic theories were expounded. The master was tolerant because the servant was diligent in the performance of his duties. Suddenly the valet stopped going to meetings, and after several weeks the master became curious enough to ask the reason.

"At the last meeting I attended," said the good man, "it was proved that if all the wealth in the country were divided equally among all the people, the share of each person would be two thousand francs."

"So what?" asked the master.

"Well, I have five thousand francs."

Wearing apparel. See Attire

Wedding anniversary

976. The most impressive evidence of tolerance is a golden wedding anniversary.

Witness—Witnesses

977. The attorney demanded severely, "You testify that you saw the defendant strike the complaining witness, and yet you were three blocks away. Just how far can you see, anyhow?"

"Oh, I don't know exactly," the witness drawled, "about a million miles, I expect—just how far away is the moon?"

978. "Mr. Witness, you're not telling the same story now that you did right after the shooting happened, are you?"

"No, sir."

"Well, how do you explain the difference?"

"Well," replied the witness, "I was talkin' then; I'm swearin' now."

Wolf—Wolves

979. Many a man works hard to keep the wolf from his door. Then his daughter grows up and brings one right into the house.

980. There was a wolf who was so poor that he couldn't afford etchings so he asked the girl friend up to see the handwriting on the wall.

Woman—Women

981. Women do not believe everything they hear—but this doesn't prevent them from repeating it.

982. There are three kinds of women. Those one cannot live without, those one cannot live with—and those one lives with.

983. A reporter was interviewing Sir Winston Churchill.

"What do you say, Sir," he asked, "to the prediction that in the year 2000, women will be ruling the world?"

Churchill smiled his wise old cherub smile, "They still will, eh?"

984. A pretty young sophomore arrived home breathlessly to announce that she had received the first of a new type of comprehensive report card at high school.

"It's got all kinds of statistics and stuff on it," she informed her mother as she handed it over for inspection. "Look at this," she exclaimed, pointing to one particular item. "They gave me an 'F' in sex and I didn't even know I was taking it."

World, The

985. If the world is getting smaller, why do they keep raising postal rates?

986. "I'll make a suit for you," agreed Ben, an overworked tailor, "but it won't be ready for 30 days."

The customer was shocked. "Thirty days," he protested. "Why, the good Lord only took 6 days to create the entire world."

"True," the tailor agreed, "but have you a taken a good look at it lately?"

Worry—Worries

987. *Contractor:* "Did you hear about Willard the bank cashier, stealing fifty-thousand and running away with nis friend's wife?"

Engineer: "Good heavens! Who'll teach his Sunday school class tomorrow?"

988. A man was complaining of insomnia. "Even counting sheep is no good. I counted 10,000, sheared 'em, combed the wool, had it spun into cloth, made into suits, took 'em into town—and lost $21 on the deal. So I haven't slept for a week."

989.   The fighter, after taking the full count in a late round of a brawl, finally came to as his handlers worked over him in the dressing room. As his head cleared and he realized what had happened, he said to his manager: "Boy, did I have him worried in the third round! He thought he'd killed me."

Youth

990. During a rehearsal of one of his plays, Sir James M. Barrie became increasingly irritated with the producer's young son, who was convinced that he knew it all.

Repeatedly, the youth interrupted the proceedings to criticize one of the principals. After one such outburst, Barrie turned to him and said:

"My boy, you will have to be more patient with us. After all we are not young enough to know everything."

DEFINITIONS

A

Ability: what will get you to the top if the boss has no daughter.

Abstract art: the proof that things are not as bad as they are painted to be.

Adam: the first white slave.

Adolescence: the age when a girl's voice changes from no to yes.

Adolescence—Middle age: Adolescence: when you think you will live forever; Middle age: when you wonder how you have lasted so long.

Adult education: a strenuous effort to learn about things that bored you when you were still young enough to profit from them.

Alimony: that which enables a woman who at one time lived happily married to live happily unmarried.

Apartment building: a place where the landlord and the tenant are both trying to raise the rent.

Apprehension, Groundless: See Groundless apprehension.

Archaeologist: a man whose career lies in ruins.

Archaeology: the science of digging around to find another civilization to blame ours on.

Art, Abstract. See Abstract art.

Astronaut: one who is glad to be down and out.

Automation: man's effort to make work so easy that women can do it all.

Average: the poorest of the good and the best of the bad.

B

B.A.: a degree which indicates that the holder has mastered the first two letters of the alphabet . . . backwards.

Bachelor: 1. a man whom no girl has maneuvered into a situation where she can say, "Yes." 2. a fellow who never finds out how many faults he has. 3, a man who has taken many a girl out but has never been taken in.

Backseat driver: a driver who drives the driver.

Balanced meal: one from which the diner has a fifty-fifty chance of recovery.

Banquet: an affair at which a man may insist that he isn't much of a speaker, then gets up and spends an hour and a half trying to prove it.

Bargain: something you figure out a use for after you've bought it.

Baseball: a pane killer.

Baseball dugout: a whine cellar.

Baseball umpire: See **Umpire**.

Bathing suit: a garment cut to see level.

Biscuit dough: a primitive adhesive used extensively and successfully by brides to prevent loss of their wedding bands.

Black eye: a stamp of disapproval.

Bookie: a fellow who makes his living off bet bugs.

Bore: 1. a guy, who, if you ask him what time it is, will start to tell you how to make a watch. 2. a person who takes his time taking your time. 3. one who need not repeat himself because he gets it trite the first time. 4. a person who is too generous with his time.

Borrower: a person who always wants to be left a loan.

Boss: 1. a fellow who'll raise the roof before he'll raise your salary. 2. the guy who watches the clock during the coffee break.

Boxing: guided muscle.

Bride: a gal who puts her foot down as soon as her new husband has carried her over the threshold.

Bridegroom: a man who is amazed at the outcome of what he thought was a harmless little flirtation.

Bum: a man-about-town.

Bumblebee: a humbug.

Bumper crop: pedestrians who land in the hospital because of automobile accidents.

C

Candidate, Political: a modest man who shrinks from the publicity of private life to seek the obscurity of public office.

Career girl: one who gets a man's salary without marrying one.

Champion: a fellow who gets licked two or three times a week and keeps right on calling himself a champion.

Chaperoning: a spectator spoil-sport.

Chess: 1. a game requiring patience, a mathematical mind, and a suit with two pairs of pants. 2. a game played on squares by squares.

Chiropractor: a doctor who works his fingers to the bone . . . yours.

Christmas: 1. that time of the year when mother has to separate the man from the toys. 2. that time of the year when both trees and husbands get trimmed, and sometimes get lit up, too. 3. a season of anticipation, preparation, recreation, relation, prostration and recuperation.

Clever woman: one who knows how to give a man her own way.

Coal: a lumpy substance that not only goes to the buyer, but to the cellar as well.

Cocktail party: where you make new old friends.

College: an institution where you learn how to use punctuation marks, but not what to put between them.

College professor: a man who gets what's left over after the football coach is paid off.

Communism: 1. the cause that suppresses. 2. Socialism with a gun to make you take it.

Commuter: one who spends his life; in riding to and from his wife; a man who shaves and takes a train; and then rides back to shave again.

Compromise: listening to your wife's opinion and deciding she's right.

Confidence: that quality which permits an individual to do crossword puzzles with a fountain pen.

Confirmed bachelor: a man with no wife expectancy.

Con man: one who believes people are all right—if you know how to take them.

Conscience: something that no's what's wrong.

Contented husband: one who is on listening terms with his wife.

Cosmetics: applied art.

Co-wed: a gal who got her man while in college.

Credit card: the greatest development since the invention of the big wheel.

D

Daily double: work and slave.

Dark corner: a place where men get bright ideas.

Debutante: a girl who's in all day and out all night.

Dentist: one who "tickles the ivories."

Diamond: one of the hardest substances known to man—especially to get back.

Diaper: a changeable seat cover.

Diary: penned-up emotion.

Diploma: a job-hunting license.

Diplomacy: 1. the art of saying nothing nicely. 2. the art of saying something when you have nothing to say, or of saying nothing when you have something to say.

Diplomat: one who can keep his shirt on while getting something off his chest.

Discharged record spinner: a slipped disc jockey.

Discretion: when you are sure that you are right but still ask your wife.

Divorce: a splitting headache.

Doghouse: falling-out shelter.

Dogma: a canine parent.

Do-it-yourself enthusiast: a varnishing American.

Domestic harmony: music produced only if the husband plays second fiddle.

Double-crosser: a man who acts like a skunk and hopes nobody will get wind of it.

Dreams: the fool ideas of the day before yesterday that have become the commonplace miracles of today.

Drinking: something which makes one lose his inhibitions and give exhibitions.

Driver, Backseat: See **Backseat driver.**

Drug, Miracle: See **Miracle drug.**

Dude ranch: where a guy who is rich enough to drive a Cadillac rides a horse.

Dugout, Baseball: See **Baseball dugout.**

Dumb babe: one who counts on her fingers instead of her legs.

E

Easy street: the route of all evil.

Eavesdropper: a woman who loves to listen in, but not as much as she loves to talk out.

Economist: a man who can save money by cutting down some other person's expense.

Education: 1. what you have left over when you subtract what you've forgotten from what you learned. 2. a technique employed to open minds so that they may go from cocksure ignorance to thoughtful uncertainty.

Egotism: self-intoxication.

Electrocardiograph: ticker tape.

Epitaph: a monumental lie.

Evolution: what makes the chimpanzee in the zoo ask: "Am I my brother's keeper?"

Executive: a person who follows his work schedule to a tee.

Experience: what you imagine you have until you get more.

Expert: one who knows all the answers, if you ask the right questions.

F

Failure: one who never puts things over because he is always putting things off.

Failures: the battle scars of those who tried.

Farmer, U. S. variety: the only man who can lose money every year, live well, educate his children, and then die rich.

Fear: the lengthened shadow of ignorance.

Fence: the difference between one yard and two yards.

Financial wizard: the man who doesn't need some extra money at Christmas time.

Flatterer: one who convinces you that you are not alone in the way you feel about yourself.

Fore: a golf bawl.

Fox: a chicken who gets a mink from a wolf.

Fox hunting: the unspeakable after the uneatable.

G

Genius: 1. a crackpot who hit the jackpot. 2. a parent who can help his kids do their homework. 3. someone shrewd enough and lazy enough to do the things right the first time. 4. a man who can talk his boss into giving him a raise . . . and his wife into letting him keep it.

Gold-digger: 1. a woman who pulls the wool over a man's eyes and then fleeces him. 2. a tomato that needs a lot of lettuce.

Golf: a certain something that depreciates when it's above par.

Golfer: a guy who hits and tells.

Good breeding: that quality that enables a person to wait in well-mannered silence while the loud mouth gets the service.

Good neighbor: one who makes his noise at the same time you make yours.

Good toastmaster: one who knows when to pop up and when to pop down.

Gossip: 1. one who usually gets caught in her own mouth-trap. 2. cheat-chat. 3. something heard over the sour grapevine.

Gossip columnist: one who writes other's wrongs.

Graduate school: the place where a young scholar goes off his dad's payroll—and on to his wife's.

Grouch: one who distrusts people who flatter him and dislikes people who don't.

Groundless apprehension: that uneasy feeling right after the plane takes off.

H

Harmony, Domestic: See **Domestic harmony.**

H-bomb: an invention to end all inventions.

Highbrow: a person who can listen to the *William Tell* overture without thinking of the *Lone Ranger*.

Home: a place a man goes to raise a fuss because something went wrong at the office.

Homework: skull-drudgery.

Hooky: when a small boy lets his mind wander—and then follows it.

Horse: an oatsmobile.

Hospital: a place where people who are run down wind up.

Human being: a guy who'll laugh over a family album, then look into a mirror and never crack a smile.

Human brain: a wonderful mechanism that starts functioning the minute you get up in the morning and doesn't stop until you get to the office.

Humility: the ability to act ashamed when you tell people how wonderful you are.

Humor: 1. emotional chaos remembered in tranquility. 2. a smoke screen that keeps us from being blinded by the truth.

Hunting, Fox: See **Fox hunting.**

Husband: a domesticated wolf.

Husband, Contented: See **Contented husband.**

Husband-hunting: a sport in which the animal that gets caught has to buy the license.

Hypochondriac: a woman who always broods over her health, but never hatches a remedy.

Hypocrite: a guy who isn't himself on Sundays.

Hypodermic needle: a sick shooter.

I

Idiot: a man who sees your point in an argument but refuses to see your way.

Impossible: what nobody can do until somebody does it.

Impressario: the only man who never suffers in the long run.

Income tax: the first touch of spring.

Infinity: a kind of foreverness that begins when a speaker says, "and in conclusion."

Inflation: a period when two can live as steeply as one.

Insanity: grounds for divorce in some states; grounds for marriage in all.

Intellectual: a guy who can keep his mind on a book at a bathing beach.

Intersection: a place where two wrongs make a rite.

Intuition: feminine radar.

Invest: a word which comes before investigate in the dictionary, but which follows it in practice.

Irish: an English-piquing people.

Irony: being witty at all costs.

J

Jail: the original key club.

Juvenile delinquent: a youngster who has been given a free hand but not in the proper place.

K

Killing time: suicide on the installment plan.

Know-it-all: one who pretends to know something about everything but really knows nothing about anything.

L

Las Vegas: 1. a place where men get chip-wrecked. 2. a place where wheels steer people.

Lawyer: a cat that settles differences between mice.

Life: the garment we continually alter but which never seems to fit.

Lingerie: gay nighties.

Lisp: to call a spade thpade.

Listening: silent flattery.

Literary tea: a fete worse than death.

Love: 1. passing fiance. 2. a word made up of two vowels, two consonants, and two fools.

M

Marriage: 1. a ceremony where the grocer acquires an account the florist once had. 2. a ceremony in which a woman gives the best years of her life to the man who made them. 3. a process whereby love ripens into vengeance. 4. an investment that pays you dividends if you pay interest. 5. oceans of emotions surrounded by expanses of expenses. 6. a very expensive way to get your laundry done free.

Masseur: a limberjack.

Maternity dress: a kind of magic garment that makes the heir unapparent.

Matrimony: the splice of life.

Meal, Balanced: See Balanced meal.

Mean precipitation: rain falling on Easter bonnets.

Middle age: when your past is past.

Minister: a travel agent for the straight and narrow.

Minute: that period of time in which, after keeping her husband waiting for an hour, a woman still promises to be ready.

Miracle drug: any medicine you can get the kids to take without screaming.

Misnomer: the right name for the wrong word.

Moderns: people who meet a crisis face to face after taking a pill.

Modesty: that self-confident feeling that the world already knows or will soon find out.

Money: what we spend for luxuries and owe for necessities.

Monotony: a system that allows a man only one wife.

Mundane: the day following a heavenly weekend.

Music lover, Real: See Real music lover.

N

Nature lover: a person who, when treed by a bear, enjoys the view.

Neurotic-Psychotic: Neurotic: a person who builds castles in the air; Psychotic: someone who moves into them.

Night gown: a nap sack.

Nuclear physicist: one who has many ions in the fire.

O

Obsolescence: what happens to your car once it's paid for.

Office picnic: when the boss goes on his vacation.

Office-seeker: a person who is either appointed or disappointed.

Old age: that time of life when you don't care where your wife goes, just so you don't have to go with her.

Old fashioned girl: one who hasn't the slightest idea what an old-fashioned is.

Old-timer: 1. one who can remember when the village square was a place—not a person. 2. one who can remember when the wonder drugs were mustard plasters and castor oil. 3. one who can remember when you built your garage on top of your house and called it an "attic."

Onion: a vegetable that builds you up physically but tears you down socially.

Optimist: one who, when he falls in the soup, considers himself in the swim.

Optimist, True: See **True optimist**.

Orator: an unpopular wind instrument.

Originality: a pair of fresh eyes.

P

Parable: a heavenly story with no earthly meaning.

Parking lot attendant: professional fender bender.

Parking meter: 1. an automatic device that bets a dollar to your nickel that you can't get back before the red flag flips up. 2. a device that makes you do two hours shopping in one.

Parking space: a place occupied by someone already there.

Patience: a postponed temper.

Patriotism: the frustration you feel when a foreigner wins the championship.

Pedestrian: 1. a husband who didn't think the family had any need for two cars. 2. a man who dies with his boots on.

Peroxide blonde: convertible top.

Pessimist: 1. one who complains about the noise when opportunity knocks. 2. one to whom every year is a good whine year. 3. a mis-fortune teller.

Phone booth: where one sees the handwriting on the wall.

Physicist, Nuclear: See **Nuclear physicist.**

Plagiarism: taking something from one man and making it worse.

Playboy, Society: See **Society playboy.**

Police: the only people who are paid to go around pinching people in the wrong places.

Political candidate: See **Candidate, Political.**

Politician: 1. a man who will stand for anything that he thinks will leave him sitting pretty. 2. a man who works his gums before an election and gums up the works afterward.

Polygon: a dead parrot.

Popeye: what some bathing beauties do to men at the beaches.

Practical man: one who looks for a wife who has a fur coat already and has had her appendix out.

Precipitation, Mean: See **Mean precipitation.**

Predicament: when a woman doesn't want any more birthdays, but still wants the presents.

Press agent: one who is willing to put your feat in his mouth.

Progress: the continuing effort to make the things we eat, drink and wear as good as we think they used to be.

Propaganda: what the other side is lying about.

Prosperity: something you feel, fold and forward to Washington.

Psychiatrist: a head coach.

Psychiatrist's couch: bunk bed.

R

Radish: a vegetable that speaks for itself.

Ranch, Dude: See Dude ranch.

Real music lover: the woman who applauds when her husband comes home singing at dawn.

Recession: what happens when the boom is lowered.

Refrigerator: where you put dabs of food on dishes you don't want to wash.

Repartee: glib and take.

Resourceful woman: one who teaches the children to swim while waiting for the plumber.

Rhetoric: language in white tie, high hat, and tails.

Rural areas: those backward places that use a substance called money rather than credit cards.

S

Sailor: a wolf in ship's clothing.

Sales talk: trade wind.

School, Graduate: See Graduate school.

Secret: something a woman tells everybody not to tell anybody.

Sermon: a moralogue.

Sewing circle: a group of women who needle each other.

Shoplifting: free enterprise.

Shotgun wedding: a case of wife or death.

Silence: the only thing that can't be misquoted.

Small town: 1. a place where nothing happens every minute. 2. a place where a person with a private phone is considered anti-social.

Smuggler: one who neglects his duty to his country.

Snob: a fellow who invents ancestors who would have been ashamed of him if they had been real.

Society playboy: a cashanova.

Soft soap: a sort of make-up cream.

Spanking: stern punishment.

Spare tire: the one you check after you have a flat.

Spinster: 1. nature's frozen asset. 2. a woman who spends her life in solitary refinement.

Spring fever: the disinclination of the sap to rise.

Stalemate: a husband with one joke.

Statistician: a person who believes that if you put your head in a furnace and your feet in a bucket of iced water, on the average you should feel reasonably comfortable.

Stenographer: a girl you pay to learn to spell while she's looking for a husband.

Stoplight: a place where the cautious and the reckless meet.

Strip teaser: one who makes a bare living.

Success: 1. the realization of the estimate which you place upon yourself. 2. the good fortune that comes from aspiration, desperation, perspiration, and inspiration.

Successful man: one who can lay a firm foundation with the bricks that others throw at him.

Summer: that time of the year when you feel so lazy, you can't get out of your own way.

Summertime: when parents pack off their troubles to an old Indian camp and smile, smile, smile!

Sympathy: what one usually gives to a friend or relative when he doesn't want to lend him money.

T

Tabloid: a screamlined newspaper.

Tax, Income: See **Income tax.**

Tea, Literary: See **Literary tea.**

Television set: a watching machine.

Tension: the price you pay for being a race horse instead of a plow horse.

Theory: 1. an educated hunch; 2. an impractical plan for doing the impossible.

Time, Killing: See **Killing time.**

Tire, Spare: See **Spare tire.**

Toastmaster: the fellow between the meal and the speaker who tries to pretend that the latter won't be as much torture as the former.

Toastmaster, Good: See **Good toastmaster.**

Tolerance: letting other people find happiness in their way instead of your way.

True optimist: one who always has his bad breaks relined.

U

Umpire: the original strike arbitrator.

V

Vacation: 1. a change of routine that makes you feel good enough to go back to work and poor enough to have to. 2. a brief relief without the chief.

Vision: looking farther than you can see.

Vocabulary, Woman's: See Woman's vocabulary.

W

Wastebasket: something to throw things near.

Wedding rehearsal: aisle trial.

Wedding ring: a warhoop.

Wedding, Shotgun: See Shotgun wedding.

Widowhood: the proof that women live longer than men.

Wig: a convertible top.

Will contest: heir splitting.

Wisdom: knowing the difference between pulling your weight and throwing it around.

Wizard: a man who can describe—without gestures—an accordion, a spiral staircase or a girl.

Wolf: a big dame hunter.

Woman: 1. a delusion men like to hug. 2. a creature who is either making a fool out of a man, or making a man out of a fool.

Woman, Clever: See Clever woman.

Woman, Resourceful: See Resourceful woman.

Woman's vocabulary: one that is small but with a big turnover.

Women: people who can talk their way out of anything but a telephone booth.

Woodpecker: a knocking bird.

World history: scrap book.

Y

Yacht: a floating debt.

Yawn: opening one's mouth and wishing that others would close theirs.

Youth: a good substitute for experience.

Z

Zoo: a place of refuge where wild animals are protected from people.

GENERAL INDEX

(Numbers in the index refer to selections
in the text, not to page numbers)

A

Abbreviation—Abbreviations, 607
Abdomen, 248
Absence, 190, 194, 252, 266, 824
Absent-mindedness, *1, 2*
Abstainer, Total, 257
Abstinence, 257
Abuse—Abusiveness, 642
Acceleration, 19
Accelerator, 157
Accent—Accents, 656
Accident—Accidents, 368
Accident, Automobile, 546
Accomplishment—Accomplishments, 907
Accord, 442
Accountant—Accountants, 471
Accuracy, *3, 4*
Accusation—Accusations, 160
Achievement—Achievements, *5,* 907
Acquaintance, New,—Acquaintances, New, 367
Action, 116
Actor—Actors, 172, 570, 875
Actor's Club, 147
Actress—Actresses, 507, 549
Adams, John Quincy, 685
Addition (Mathematics), 33
Address—Addresses, 898
Adenauer, Konrad, 22
Admiral—Admirals, 580
Admiration, *6*
Admission, Guilt, 917
Advancement, 291
Advance payment, 412
Advantage—Advantages, 750
Advertisement—Advertisements, 353, 434, 658
Advertising, *7–11,* 303, 882
Advice, 62, 72, 495, 637, 784
Advisor, Vocational, 964
Africa, 416, 485, 600
After-dinner speaker—After-dinner speakers, 727
Age, *12–17,* 135, 325, 364, 771
Age, Comparative, 13
Agent, Insurance,—Agents, Insurance, 480
Aging, *18–23,* 536, 713

Agriculture, 165
Aim, 264
Air-conditioning, 29
Airplane—Airplanes, 592
Airport—Airports, 411, 592, 940
Air travel, 940
Alarm clock—Alarm clocks, 318
Alcoholic liquor, 23, 31, 89, 98, 100, 185, 261, 294, 578, 585, 612, 748, 823
Alimony, 550
Allegation—Allegations, 502
Allen, George E., 684
Allen, John, 673
Alma Mater, 775
Alternative—Alternatives, 519
Alumni, College, 589, 621
Amateur—Amateurs, 737
Ambassador—Ambassadors, 541, 732
Ambition, 699
Ambulance chasing, 451
America—Americanism, *24,* 82, 162, 469, 882, 945
American—Americans, 127, 145, 160, 162, 516, 518, 648, 656, 948
American industry, 291
American Psychological Association, 864
American Society for the Prevention of Cruelty to Animals, 744
Amputation—Amputations, 606
Anaesthetic, 243
Anaesthetic, Local, 241
Ancestry, *25, 26*
Ancient history, 34
Ancient temple—Ancient temples, 433
Anderson, Clinton, 736
And/or, 519
Anecdote—Anecdotes, 485
Angel—Angels, 609
Anger, *27,* 169, 628, 808
Animal—Animals, 396, 508
Anniversary celebration, 294
Anniversary, Wedding,—Anniversaries, Wedding, *976*
Annoyance, 287, 373
Annual dinner—Annual dinners, 971
Ant—Ants, 693
Anticipation, 55, 378
Antique—Antiques, *28*
Antique shop—Antique shops, 666

Bank—Banks—Banking, *82–85*, 111, 270, 324
Bank cashier—Bank cashiers, 987
Bank check—Bank checks, 79, 83
Bank deposit—Bank deposits, 909
Bank director—Bank directors, 970
Banker—Bankers, 290
Bankruptcy, 63, 212, 270, 301
Bank teller—Bank tellers, 909
Banquet—Banquets, 69, 682
Baptism, 678
Bar—Bars, 258, 260, 443
Barber—Barber shop, 80, *86–90*
Bargain—Bargains, *91–93*, 175
Bargaining, 657, 706, 816
Bark—Barking, 161, 828
Barn—Barns, 51, 309, 513
Barnacle—Barnacles, 493
Barracks, Army, 44, 884
Barrel—Barrels, 120
Barrie, James M., 990
Barrister—Barristers, 303
Barroom—Barrooms, 213
Bartender—Bartenders, 213, 266, 748
Baseball—Baseballs, 183, 232, 865, 869
Baseball bat—Baseball bats, 183
Baseball player—Baseball players, 782
Basketball—Basketballs, 449
Bassinet—Bassinets, 274
Bathe—Bathing, 579
Bathing beauty—Bathing beauties, 619
Bathing suit—Bathing suits, 211
Bathrobe—Bathrobes, 955
Bathroom—Bathrooms, 411, 463, 576, 579, 628, 929
Bathtub—Bathtubs, 873, 910
Beach—Beaches, 30, 572, 619
Bear—Bears, 746
Beard—Beards, 66, 617, 875
Beast—Beasts, 167, 222
Beauty, *94, 95*, 631, 787
Beaver—Beavers, 683
Bed pan—Bed pans, 651
Bedroll—Bedrolls, 640
Bedroom—Bedrooms, 235
Beecher, Henry Ward, 881
Beer, 403
Beethoven, Ludwig van, 6
Beg—Begging, 261
Behavior, *96–100*
Bell—Bells, 660
Bellboy, Hotel, 411, 923
Bellhop—Bellhops, 926
Belongings, 77
Beneficiary—Beneficiaries, 533
Benevolent Protective Order of Elks, 414

Bequest—Bequests, 361, 464
"Berth Control," 109
Berth, Pullman, 573
Best man, 708
Bet—Bets—Betting. See also Gambling, *101, 102*, 111, 395, 400
Beverly Hills, California, 703
Bible, The, *103*, 461, 562, 565
Bicarbonate of soda, 335, 702
Bicycle—Bicycles, 30
Bifocal spectacles, 380
Bigotry, 257
Bikini—Bikinis, 211, 619
Bill—Bills, 208, 263, 505, 879
Billious, 611
Biology, 174
Bird—Birds, 791
Birth, 800
Birthday—Birthdays, 336
Birthday celebration, 357
Birthday gift—Birthday gifts, 66, 143, 461
Birth rate, 105
Bishop—Bishops, 225, 840
Bite—Biting, 811
Blackboard—Blackboards, 514
Blackguard—Blackguards, 523
Blame, *104, 105*, 260, 292, 433, 554
Blanket—Blankets, 573
Blanket, Electric,—Blankets, Electric, 557
Bleached hair, 218
Blindness, 164, 865
Blinds, Window, 873
Block, Concrete,—Blocks, Concrete, 219
Blonde—Blondes, 211, 785, 831
Bluff—Bluffing, 125
Bluntness, 883
Board of health, 934
Boastfulness, *106–108*, 191, 317, 416
Boat—Boats, 110
Body, Human, 646
Bomb, Hydrogen, 215
Bonus—Bonuses, 925
Bonus, Christmas, 301
Book—Books, *109, 110*, 250, 461, 689, 947, 974
Bookie—Bookies, 102
Bookkeeper—Bookkeepers, 477
Bookkeeping, 85, 290, 300
Boomerang—Boomerangs, 339
Booze. See also Alcoholic liquor, 98, 261
Border—Borders, 158
Bore—Bores, 543

D

Damnation, 225
Dance—Dances, 454
Dancing, 99, *200–202*, 757, 761
Danger—Dangers, 647, 732
Darkness, 812
Date—Dating, 298
Daughter—Daughters, 211, 979
Day—Days, 224
Daytime, 249
Dead, 934
Deadbeat—Deadbeats, 476
Deafness, 202
Deal, Business,—Deals, Business, 927
Death, 216, 266, 288, 504, 647, 757
Death sentence, 225
Debate—Debates, 668
Debt—Debts, *203, 204,* 209, 366, 476, 879
Debtor—Creditor, 194, *205–213,* 244
Decalogue, The, 103, 314
Deceased estate, 701
Deception, *214*
Decision—Decisions, 310, 685
Decode—Decoding, 580
Deductibility, 359
Defalcation, 85, 300
Defeat—Defeats, 512, 682, 685
Defendant—Defendants, 303
Defensive play—Defensive plays, 867
Deference, 11
Delay, 255
Delinquency, Juvenile, 635
Delivery boy—Delivery boys, 312
Delusion—Delusions, 214, 717
Democracy, *215*
Democratic party, 730
Democrat, Western,—Democrats, Western, 164
Denial, 678
Denomination, Religious, 346
Dentist—Dentists, 190, 620, 690, 700, 880
Department head—Department heads, 298
Department store—Department stores, 300, 937
Dependent clause, 164
Depew, Chauncey, 257, 487
Deposit—Deposits, 476
Deposit slip, Bank,—Deposit slips, Bank, 909
Depravity, 625
Depreciation, 816
Desertion, Marital, 372

Dessert—Desserts, 223, 585
Destination, *216, 217,* 905
Destroyer, Naval, 580
Destruction, 58
Detective—Detectives, 662, 956
Detective, House,—Detectives, House, 171
Devil, The, 137, 214, 521
Devos, Raymond, 721
Dewey, Thomas E., 669, 682
Diagnosis, *218–220,* 647, 715
Diagnostic examination, 706
Diamond—Diamonds, 564
Diamond ring—Diamond rings, 437
Diaper—Diapers, 548, 669
Dictation, Letter, 106, 857
Dictionary—Dictionaries, 324, 836, 861
Diet—Dieting. See also Overweight, *221–223,* 244, 619
Difference—Differences, 97, 173, *224–226,* 351, 388, 517, 810, 869, 963
Dignitary—Dignitaries, 485
Dining, 99
Dining room—Dining rooms, 235, 818
Dinner guest—Dinner guests, 406, 972
Dinosaur—Dinosaurs, 4
Diplomacy, 106
Diplomat—Diplomats, 541
Direction—Directions, *227–229,* 938, 970
Direct-mail campaign, 827
Disadvantage—Disadvantages, 750
Disappearance, 420
Disappointment—Disappointments, 155, *230–232,* 659, 685
Discard, 339
Discharge, Employment, 298, 300, 623
Discomfort, 457
Disconcern, 170
Discordance, 6
Discovery, 146
Disease—Diseases, 256
Dish—Dishes, 201, 650, 902
Dishwashing, 145, 425, 572
Dishwater, 564
Disillusionment, 621
Disinterest, 959
Disobedience, 639
Disrespect, 642
Disruption, Conversation, 177
Dissatisfaction, 204
Distance—Distances, 912, 977
District attorney—District attorneys, 966

J

Jackass–Jackasses, 676
Jackson, Andrew, 676
Jail–Jails, 160, 197, 217, 507, 522, 917
Jefferson, Thomas, 685
Jesus, 691, 742
Jewelry, 300, 478
Jewish holiday, 226
J.F.K., 607
Jilt–Jilted, 721
Job, 565
Job applicant–Job applicants, 312
Joint account–Joint accounts, 113
Joint effort, *490–492*
Joint ownership, 77
Joke–Jokes, 310
Jones, Ben, 529
Journalism. See also Newspaper–
    Newspapers, 100, 114, 115, 176,
    493–502
Journalism school–Journalism schools,
    502
Journalist–Journalists, 695
Judge–Judges, 14, 225, 456, 506
Judge, Federal,–Judges, Federal, 584
Judgeship, 584
Jungle–Jungles, 146, 746
Jurisdiction, *503, 504*
Jury–Juries, 709
Justice, *505–507*
Justice of the peace, 764
Juvenile delinquency, 635

K

Kennedy, John F., 607
Kennel–Kennels, 25
Kentucky, State of, 322
Ketchup, 10
Key–Keys, 614
Key, Automobile, 614
Kick–Kicking, 508, 891
Kieran, John, 968
Killarney, Eire, 393
Kilt–Kilts, 393
Kindergarten–Kindergartens, 628
Kindness, *508, 509*
King John (England), 25
Kirkpatrick, C. W., 139
Kiss–Kisses–Kissing, 1, 357, 484,
    510. 511 811

Kitchen–Kitchens, 178, 235, 692
Kitchen appliance–Kitchen
    appliances, 590
Kitchen sink–Kitchen sinks, 572
Kitten–Kittens, 164, 599
Knick-Knack–Knick-Knacks, 357
Knife–Knives, 180
Knit–Knitting, 610, 813
Know-how, *512–514*
Knowledge, 61, 243, 417, 877, 911

L

Label–Labels, 872
Laboratory–Laboratories, 961
Labor union–Labor unions, 290, 582
Labrador–Labradors, 227
Lace, 759
Ladder–Ladders, 696
Ladle–Ladles, 54
Lamb–Lambs, 150
Landlord–Tenant, *515, 516*
Landslide, Political, 670
Language, *517, 518*
Language, French, 641
Lantern–Lanterns, 332
Larceny, 194, 525, 526, 662, 710
La Scala Opera House, 648
Las Vegas, Nevada, 16, 61, 343-345
Late hours, 245
Laughing gas, 690
Laughter, 549
Laundry, 753
Laundry list–Laundry lists, 466
Lavatory–Lavatories, 227, 751
Law–Laws, 507
Lawn–Lawns, 355, 743, 815
Lawn mower, Power,–Lawn mowers,
    Power, 355
Law, Obedience to, 186
Law practice, 520
Law, Retroactive,–Laws, Retroactive,
    559
Lawsuit–Lawsuits, 521, 524, 528,
    546
Lawyer–Lawyers, 162, 272, 303, 344,
    451, 456, *519–521,* 585, 672,
    977
Lawyer–Client, 233, *522–528,* 699
Laziness, *529, 530,* 623
Leading lady–Leading ladies, 583
Leak–Leaks, 170
Leakage, Plumbing, 576
Learning, 7, 641

Wealth, 241, 250, 322, 535, 551, 804, 920, 924, *974, 975*
Wearing apparel, 133, 608, 609, 626, 664, 773, 832, 879, 951
Weather, 832
Weather prediction, 383
Weather prophet—Weather prophets, 383
Webster, Daniel, 73, 483
Wedding—Weddings, 708
Wedding anniversary—Wedding anniversaries, *976*
Wedding ceremony—Wedding ceremonies, 503, 741
Wedding march, 779
Wedding ring—Wedding rings, 564
Wedding, Society,—Weddings, Society, 497
"We," Editorial, 494
Weed—Weeds, 351
Weight, Loss of, 627
Welcome sign, 134
Welfare fund, 967
Welshman—Welshmen, 79
Western Democrats, 164
Westerner—Westerners, 401
Western Union, 846
West Germany, 22
Wheelbarrow—Wheelbarrows, 936
Whereabouts, 165
Whiskey punch, 257
Whistle—Whistling, 48
White man—White men, 169
Widow—Widows, 445, 885
Widower—Widowers, 445
Wife—Wives, 186, 224, 248, 269, 327, 565, 752, 951
Willingness, 7
Will, Testamentary, 464, 532, 535, 757
Wind, 750
Window—Windows, 29, 736
Window blinds, 873
Window shade—Window shades, 171
Windscreen, 518
Windshield—Windshields, 518
Wine—Wines, 156, 402
Winter—Winters, 732, 831, 947, 954
Withdrawal, Funds, 113
Withholding tax—Withholding taxes, 967

Witness—Witnesses, 710, *977, 978*
Witness box, 14
Witness oath, 14
Wolf—Wolves, 363, 581, 800, *979, 980*
Wolfhound, Russian,—Wolfhounds, Russian, 161
Woman—Women, 12, 98, 156, 626, 831–833, 939, *981–984*
Wooden-head, 41
Woodpile, 392
Word—Words, 809
Work, 623
Workhouse, 507
World, Creation of, 115
World, The, 203, 204, *985, 986*
World War I, 229
Worm—Worms, 307
Worry—Worries, 269, 464, *987–989*
Wright, Frank Lloyd, 170

X

X-Ray specialist—X-Ray specialists, 741

Y

Yacht—Yachts, 300, 523
Yankee—Yankees, 67
Yellowstone National Park, 830
Yolk, Egg,—Yolks, Egg, 191
Youth, *990*
Youthfulness, 713

Z

Zangwill, Israel, 839
Zipper—Zippers, 694
Zoo—Zoos, 121, 150, 185, 396, 661, 901
Zoo director—Zoo directors, 150
Zoo keeper—Zoo keepers, 121